Yves Igor Jerschow

Attackers, Packets, and Puzzles

Yves Igor Jerschow

Attackers, Packets, and Puzzles

On Denial-of-Service Prevention in Local Area Networks

Südwestdeutscher Verlag für Hochschulschriften

Impressum / Imprint
Bibliografische Information der Deutschen Nationalbibliothek: Die Deutsche Nationalbibliothek verzeichnet diese Publikation in der Deutschen Nationalbibliografie; detaillierte bibliografische Daten sind im Internet über http://dnb.d-nb.de abrufbar.
Alle in diesem Buch genannten Marken und Produktnamen unterliegen warenzeichen-, marken- oder patentrechtlichem Schutz bzw. sind Warenzeichen oder eingetragene Warenzeichen der jeweiligen Inhaber. Die Wiedergabe von Marken, Produktnamen, Gebrauchsnamen, Handelsnamen, Warenbezeichnungen u.s.w. in diesem Werk berechtigt auch ohne besondere Kennzeichnung nicht zu der Annahme, dass solche Namen im Sinne der Warenzeichen- und Markenschutzgesetzgebung als frei zu betrachten wären und daher von jedermann benutzt werden dürften.

Bibliographic information published by the Deutsche Nationalbibliothek: The Deutsche Nationalbibliothek lists this publication in the Deutsche Nationalbibliografie; detailed bibliographic data are available in the Internet at http://dnb.d-nb.de.
Any brand names and product names mentioned in this book are subject to trademark, brand or patent protection and are trademarks or registered trademarks of their respective holders. The use of brand names, product names, common names, trade names, product descriptions etc. even without a particular marking in this works is in no way to be construed to mean that such names may be regarded as unrestricted in respect of trademark and brand protection legislation and could thus be used by anyone.

Coverbild / Cover image: www.ingimage.com

Verlag / Publisher:
Südwestdeutscher Verlag für Hochschulschriften
ist ein Imprint der / is a trademark of
AV Akademikerverlag GmbH & Co. KG
Heinrich-Böcking-Str. 6-8, 66121 Saarbrücken, Deutschland / Germany
Email: info@svh-verlag.de

Herstellung: siehe letzte Seite /
Printed at: see last page
ISBN: 978-3-8381-3392-8

Zugl. / Approved by: Düsseldorf, Heinrich-Heine-Universität, Diss., 2012

Copyright © 2012 AV Akademikerverlag GmbH & Co. KG
Alle Rechte vorbehalten. / All rights reserved. Saarbrücken 2012

Abstract

In this thesis, we tackle the problem of securing communication in Local Area Networks (LANs) and making it resistant against *Denial-of-Service (DoS) attacks*. The main vulnerability in wired and wireless LANs is the lack of initial address authenticity. It enables an attacker to take on different identities and to inject faked packets bearing a foreign or a bogus sender address. For this reason existing DoS countermeasures developed to mitigate attacks in the Internet have drawbacks when being applied in LANs.

Our first contribution is the *Cryptographic Link Layer (CLL)*—a comprehensive security protocol that provides authentication and confidentiality between neighboring hosts from the link layer upwards. CLL employs public-key cryptography to identify all hosts in the Ethernet LAN based on their IP/MAC address pairs. Unicast IP traffic is safeguarded by means of a block cipher and a message authentication code. CLL extends ARP and DHCP handshakes with authentication to protect these protocols against various kinds of attacks. Beginning with an ARP handshake, two hosts exchange certificates and cryptographic parameters, authenticate each other, and negotiate symmetric keys to establish a security association. CLL has been implemented on both Windows and Linux and achieves a very competitive performance.

Verifying digital signatures in the handshake phase of CLL and of other security protocols that rely on public-key cryptography is a very expensive task compared to symmetric-key operations. Thus, it may become a target for DoS attacks where the adversary floods a victim host with faked signature packets trying to overload it. We introduce a countermeasure against DoS flooding attacks on public-key handshakes in LANs, called *counter-flooding*. A benign host trying to initiate an authentication handshake to a victim system that suffers from a flooding attack reacts to this aggression by flooding itself multiple copies of its signature packet for a short period. The key idea is for the victim host to verify only a fixed number of signatures per time period without becoming overloaded and to select those packets for verification that have the largest number of duplicates. We provide bounds for counter-flooding to succeed and show experimentally that in switched Ethernet a reasonable fair bandwidth division between concurrent flows is usually ensured.

Abstract

A well-known countermeasure against resource exhaustion attacks in the Internet are client puzzles. However, existing client puzzle schemes are either parallelizable, coarse-grained, or can be used only interactively. Interactive puzzles have the drawback that the packet with the puzzle parameters sent from server to client lacks authentication. Especially in LANs the attacker can mount a counterattack on the clients by injecting packets with fake puzzle parameters that pretend to come from the defending server. We propose a novel scheme for client puzzles based on the computation of square roots modulo a prime. *Modular square root puzzles* are non-parallelizable, can be employed both interactively and particularly non-interactively, and have polynomial granularity. Benchmark results demonstrate the feasibility of our approach to mitigate DoS attacks on hosts in 1 or even 10 Gbit networks. Furthermore, the efficiency of the scheme can be raised by adding a small bandwidth-based cost factor for the client.

By introducing a *secure client puzzle architecture* we provide a solid basis to safely employ non-interactive client puzzles. It overcomes the authentication issue of interactive puzzles and prevents precomputation attacks. In our architecture, client puzzles, e.g., modular square root or hash-reversal puzzles, are employed non-interactively and constructed by the client from a periodically changing, secure *random beacon*. The beacons are generated in advance for a longer time span and regularly broadcasted in the LAN by a special beacon server. All hosts obtain a signed fingerprint package consisting of cryptographic digests of these beacons. Verifying a beacon is easy—it takes only a single hash operation and can be performed at line speed by all hosts. To guarantee a robust beacon service, we develop sophisticated techniques which address synchronization aspects and especially the secure deployment of beacon fingerprints.

In our final contribution, we pursue the idea of cryptographic puzzles beyond DoS protection and propose a novel application in the area of *timed-release cryptography*. We introduce a non-interactive and non-parallelizable *RSA time-lock puzzle* scheme where the time required to encrypt a message can be arbitrarily tuned by artificially enlarging the public exponent. Based on RSA time-lock puzzles, we present an *offline submission protocol*. It enables an author currently being offline to commit to its document before the deadline by continuously solving an RSA puzzle for that document and to submit it past the deadline just upon regaining connectivity. The correct puzzle solution serves as a proof to the accepting institution that the document in fact has been completed in time. To demonstrate the applicability of our scheme, we provide a platform-independent tool that performs all parts of our offline submission protocol.

Zusammenfassung

Diese Arbeit widmet sich dem Problem, die Kommunikation in lokalen Netzwerken (LANs) abzusichern und sie gegen *Denial-of-Service (DoS) -Angriffe* resistent zu machen. Die Hauptschwachstelle in drahtgebunden und drahtlosen LANs ist die initial fehlende Adressauthentizität. Sie ermöglicht es einem Angreifer, unterschiedliche Identitäten anzunehmen und gefälschte Pakete mit einer fremden oder fiktiven Absenderadresse einzuschleusen. Aus diesem Grund stellen sich existierende DoS-Gegenmaßnahmen, die zur Abwehr von Angriffen im Internet entwickelt worden sind, für die Anwendung in lokalen Netzwerken nur als bedingt geeignet heraus.

Der erste Beitrag ist die *kryptographische Sicherungsschicht (engl.: Cryptographic Link Layer) CLL* – ein umfassendes Sicherheitsprotokoll, welches Authentifizierung und Vertraulichkeit zwischen benachbarten Rechnern ab der Sicherungsschicht aufwärts gewährleistet. CLL setzt Public-Key-Kryptographie ein, um alle Rechner im Ethernet-LAN basierend auf ihren IP/MAC-Adresspaaren zu identifizieren. Unicast-IP-Verkehr wird mit Hilfe einer Blockchiffre und eines Nachrichtenauthentifizierungscodes abgesichert. CLL erweitert die ARP- und DHCP-Handshakes um Authentifizierungsmechanismen, um diese Protokolle vor verschiedenen Arten von Angriffen zu schützen. Beginnend mit einem ARP-Handshake tauschen zwei Rechner Zertifikate und kryptographische Parameter aus, authentifizieren sich gegenseitig und vereinbaren symmetrische Schlüssel für den Aufbau einer Sicherheitsbeziehung. CLL wurde sowohl unter Windows als auch Linux implementiert und erzielt eine sehr solide Performance.

Die Verifizierung digitaler Signaturen in der Handshake-Phase von CLL und von anderen Sicherheitsprotokollen, die Public-Key-Kryptographie einsetzen, stellt im Vergleich zu symmetrischen Kryptoverfahren eine sehr rechenaufwendige Operation dar. Daher kann sie zur Zielscheibe von DoS-Angriffen werden, in denen der Angreifer ein Opfersystem mit gefälschten Signaturen flutet und es dadurch zu überlasten versucht. Es wird eine Abwehrmaßnahme gegen DoS-Flutangriffe auf Public-Key-Handshakes in LANs entwickelt, genannt *Counter-Flooding*. Ein gutwilliger Rechner, der ein Authentifizierungshandshake zu einem System zu initiieren versucht, welches gerade Opfer eines

Zusammenfassung

Flutangriffs ist, reagiert auf diese Aggression, indem er selbst für eine kurze Zeit Kopien seines Signaturpakets flutet. Die zentrale Idee ist, dass das Opfersystem nur eine feste Anzahl an Signaturen pro Zeitabschnitt überprüft, ohne überlastet zu werden, und dabei nur diejenigen Pakete berücksichtigt, welche die größte Anzahl an Duplikaten aufweisen. Es werden Schranken für den Erfolg der Counter-Flooding-Maßnahme aufgestellt, und es wird experimentell gezeigt, dass in geswitchtem Ethernet eine hinreichend faire Bandbreitenaufteilung zwischen konkurrierenden Paketflüssen in der Regel gewährleistet ist.

Eine wohlbekannte Abwehrmaßnahme gegen Angriffe im Internet, die die Erschöpfung von Ressourcen zum Ziel haben, sind Client Puzzles. Allerdings sind die bisher vorgeschlagenen Client-Puzzle-Konstrukte entweder parallelisierbar, grobkörnig oder sie lassen sich nur interaktiv einsetzen. Interaktive Puzzles haben den Nachteil, dass das Paket mit den Puzzle-Parametern, welches vom Server zum Client geschickt wird, nicht authentifiziert wird. Insbesondere in LANs kann der Angreifer einen Gegenangriff auf die Clients starten, indem er Pakete mit falschen Puzzle-Parametern einschleust, die den Anschein erwecken, vom sich verteidigenden Server zu stammen. Es wird ein neues Konstrukt für Client Puzzles vorgeschlagen, das auf der Berechnung der Quadratwurzel modulo einer Primzahl beruht. *Modulare Quadratwurzel-Puzzles* sind nicht parallelisierbar, können sowohl interaktiv als auch insbesondere nicht interaktiv eingesetzt werden und weisen eine polynomielle Granularität auf. Benchmark-Ergebnisse untermauern die Praxistauglichkeit dieses Ansatzes, DoS-Angriffen auf Rechner in 1 oder sogar 10 Gbit Netzwerken entgegenzuwirken. Außerdem kann die Effizienz des Verfahrens durch Einführen eines kleinen bandbreitenbasierten Kostenfaktors für den Client erhöht werden.

Mit der Einführung einer *sicheren Client-Puzzle-Architektur* wird eine solide Grundlage für den zuverlässigen und wirksamen Einsatz von nicht interaktiven Client Puzzles geschaffen. Sie beseitigt das Authentifizierungsproblem von interaktiven Puzzles und beugt Vorausberechnungsangriffen vor. In der vorgeschlagenen Architektur werden Client Puzzles, z. B. modulare Quadratwurzel-Puzzles oder auf der Umkehrung einer Hashfunktion basierende Puzzles, nicht interaktiv eingesetzt und dabei vom Client aus einem sich periodisch ändernden, sicheren *zufälligen Beacon* abgeleitet. Die Beacons werden für eine längere Zeitspanne im Voraus erzeugt und im gesamten LAN von einem speziellen Beacon-Server regelmäßig per Broadcast verschickt. Alle Rechner beziehen eine digital signierte Fingerabdruck-Datei, die aus den kryptographischen Prüfsummen dieser Beacons besteht. Die Überprüfung eines Beacons ist einfach – sie erfordert lediglich eine einzige Hash-Operation und kann von allen Rechnern mit der vollen Datenrate der Netzwerkschnittstelle durchgeführt werden. Um einen stabilen Beacon-Dienst zu gewährleisten, werden ausgeklügelte Techniken entwickelt, die Synchronisierungsaspekte berücksichtigen und insbesondere die zuverlässige Verteilung der Beacon-Fingerabdruck-Datei sicherstellen.

Im letzten Beitrag wird die Idee der kryptographischen Puzzles über die DoS-Abwehr hinaus verfolgt und eine neue Anwendung auf dem Gebiet der *Timed-Release-Kryptographie* vorgeschlagen. Es wird ein nicht interaktives und nicht parallelisierbares *RSA-Time-Lock-Puzzle*-Konstrukt eingeführt, wo die Zeit, die zum Verschlüsseln einer Nachricht benötigt wird, durch künstliche Vergrößerung des öffentlichen Exponenten beliebig lang gewählt werden kann. Basierend auf RSA-Time-Lock-Puzzles wird ein *Protokoll für Offline-Einreichung* vorgestellt. Es ermöglicht es einem Autor, welcher sich gegenwärtig offline befindet, sich an sein Dokument vor Ablauf der Abgabefrist zu binden, indem er so lange ein RSA-Puzzle für dieses Dokument löst, bis die Internetkonnektivität irgendwann nach Ablauf der Abgabefrist wiedererlangt wird. Dann wird das Dokument zusammen mit der Lösung des Puzzles umgehend eingereicht. Die korrekte Lösung des Rätsels dient der Annahmestelle dabei als Beweis, dass das Dokument tatsächlich fristgerecht fertiggestellt worden ist. Zur Demonstration der praktischen Anwendbarkeit dieses Ansatzes wird ein plattformunabhängiges Tool bereitgestellt, welches alle Schritte des Offline-Einreichungsprotokolls ausführt.

Zusammenfassung

Acknowledgments

First of all, I want to express my gratitude to my doctoral advisor Martin Mauve. He invited me to join the Computer Networks Research Group at the Heinrich Heine University Düsseldorf straight after finishing my master thesis and gave me the opportunity to work on my PhD. I had the great chance to choose a challenging topic on my own while Martin Mauve continuously supported my ideas and regularly encouraged me to go into the right direction. During the last four years, he had always time to discuss the progress of my work and gave me very valuable feedback, advice, and suggestions.

The second person who had a great influence especially on my first research contributions is Björn Scheuermann. I am very grateful to him for being co-author of my first papers, for teaching me how to take the first steps in the world of research and for giving me critical but always very constructive feedback. Beginning from the time of being supervisor of my bachelor and master thesis, Björn Scheuermann was an impressive source of inspiration, insights and new ideas. It was an interesting experience to observe him on his steep path from a young PhD student over a postdoc researcher and assistant professor to a full professor.

Christian Lochert, who along with Björn Scheuermann supervised both my bachelor and master thesis and also became co-author of my first papers, deserves my gratitude as well.

My other colleagues at our chair provided me with a pleasant working atmosphere and I enjoy looking back on many interesting discussions with Daniel Baselt, Markus Koegel, Norbert Goebel, and Michael Stini. Sabine Freese, our group's secretary, handled all the necessary paperwork in the academic bureaucracy and was always very kind and helpful. Our system administrator Thomas Spitzlei was responsible for the technical support. He did his job quickly, unobtrusively, and was every time open to my questions.

Acknowledgments

I would like to thank Jörg Rothe for agreeing to be referee for this thesis. His lectures in theoretical computer science, especially in cryptography, that I attended during my study period had a special charm and became the groundwork for my later research.

Moritz Gericke and Julius Römmler contributed to this work during their bachelor thesis by extending my original implementations of CLL and OSRTLP. They performed their task very well and also deserve many thanks.

This thesis is dedicated to my mother, Tamara Jerschow. Without her I would not have achieved anything in this life and my education is her chief merit. She paved the way for me to finish school, to go to university and, finally, to write this PhD thesis. I owe my deepest gratitude to her for unconditionally supporting me with her love and advice throughout all the years. Thank you, Mom!

Contents

List of Figures . . . xv

List of Tables . . . xvii

List of Abbreviations . . . xix

1 **Introduction** . . . 1

2 **CLL: A Cryptographic Link Layer for LANs** . . . 7
   2.1 Related Work . . . 9
   2.2 Protocol Overview . . . 11
   2.3 Cryptographic Design Decisions . . . 14
   2.4 Operation of CLL in Detail . . . 15
      2.4.1 Basic Packet Format . . . 15
      2.4.2 ARP Handshake and SA Setup . . . 16
      2.4.3 Unicast IP Packets . . . 20
      2.4.4 Periodical Key Rollover . . . 21
      2.4.5 Broadcast Packets . . . 22
   2.5 Integrating and Securing DHCP . . . 23
      2.5.1 Basic Concept . . . 23
      2.5.2 Authenticating the Packets . . . 24
      2.5.3 Further Security Measures . . . 25
   2.6 Implementation and Evaluation . . . 26
      2.6.1 CLL as a Cross-Platform Service . . . 26
      2.6.2 Performance Evaluation . . . 27
      2.6.3 Gigabit Ethernet and Parallelization . . . 30
   2.7 Chapter Summary . . . 31

3 **Counter-Flooding: DoS Protection for Public-Key Handshakes in LANs** . . . 33
   3.1 Related Work . . . 35
   3.2 Design of Counter-Flooding . . . 37
      3.2.1 Goal: Safeguarding the Public-Key Handshake . . . 37
      3.2.2 Basic Idea . . . 38
      3.2.3 Bandwidth vs. Packet Count . . . 40
      3.2.4 Determining the Flooding Duration . . . 40
      3.2.5 Choosing the Parameters . . . 42
   3.3 More Details . . . 43

		3.3.1	Reducing the Queue Size	43
		3.3.2	Impact of Counter-Flooding on Network Performance	44
		3.3.3	Comparison to a Probabilistic Arbitration Scheme	44
	3.4	Flooding Experiments in Switched Ethernet		45
		3.4.1	IEEE 802.3x Flow Control	45
		3.4.2	Bandwidth Division between Host A and Attacker	46
		3.4.3	Preventing DoS Flooding Attacks on TCP	49
	3.5	Chapter Summary		50
4	**Non-Parallelizable and Non-Interactive Client Puzzles**			**51**
	4.1	Related Work		53
	4.2	Modular Square Roots		55
		4.2.1	Extracting Square Roots Modulo a Prime	55
		4.2.2	Modular Exponentiation	58
		4.2.3	Non-Parallelizability	59
	4.3	Client Puzzles from Modular Square Roots		60
		4.3.1	Constructing and Solving a Non-Interactive Puzzle	60
		4.3.2	Puzzle Verification	62
		4.3.3	Puzzle Granularity and Public Auditability	63
		4.3.4	Interactive Client Puzzles	63
		4.3.5	Client Puzzles from Modular Cube Roots?	64
	4.4	Evaluation and Protocol Enhancements		65
		4.4.1	Puzzle Benchmark	65
		4.4.2	Increasing the Bandwidth-Based Payment	68
	4.5	Chapter Summary		69
5	**Secure Client Puzzle Architecture based on Random Beacons**			**71**
	5.1	Related Work		73
	5.2	Secure Client Puzzle Architecture		74
		5.2.1	Non-Interactive Client Puzzles	74
		5.2.2	Client Puzzles from a Random Beacon	75
		5.2.3	Puzzle Construction	76
		5.2.4	Random Beacon Server	77
		5.2.5	Receiving and Verifying the Beacons	79
		5.2.6	Puzzle Submission and Verification	81
	5.3	Protocol Extensions		81
		5.3.1	Beacon Distribution across LAN Boundaries	81
		5.3.2	Emergency Deployment of Beacon Fingerprints	83
	5.4	Chapter Summary		86
6	**Offline Submission with RSA Time-Lock Puzzles**			**89**
	6.1	Related Work		91
		6.1.1	Time-Lock Puzzles	91
		6.1.2	More Timed-Release Cryptography	93
	6.2	RSA Time-Lock Puzzle Scheme		94

	6.2.1	Key Generation	94
	6.2.2	Public and Private Key Operation	95
	6.2.3	Security Analysis	96
	6.2.4	Delayed Encryption and Signature Verification	97
	6.2.5	Other Applications for RSA Time-Lock Puzzles	98
	6.2.6	Small Private Exponent	99
6.3	Offline Submission Protocol		99
	6.3.1	Basic Design	99
	6.3.2	Building a Puzzle Chain	101
	6.3.3	Alternative Approach	102
6.4	Implementation and Evaluation		102
	6.4.1	The OSRTLP Tool	102
	6.4.2	Extensions: GUI and Online Submission System	104
	6.4.3	Performance Evaluation	106
6.5	Chapter Summary		108

7 Conclusion   **109**

Bibliography   **113**

Index   **123**

Contents

List of Figures

2.1	CLL in the protocol stack.	12
2.2	An Ethernet frame in CLL.	16
2.3	ARP handshake: Diffie-Hellman key exchange in conjunction with RSA signatures.	17
2.4	Transmission of unicast IP packets safeguarded with a block cipher and a message authentication code.	21
2.5	Renegotiation—renewing an SA.	22
3.1	The counter-flooding approach.	40
3.2	Bandwidth division experiments: counter-flooding broadcast packets with parallel TCP connection (CF_B TCP).	46
6.1	Illustration of the offline submission protocol.	100
6.2	OSRTLP GUI with wizard-style interface: solving a puzzle chain.	105

List of Figures

List of Tables

2.1	Algorithms and parameters in CLL.	15
2.2	Performance of the ARP handshake.	28
2.3	Performance of unicast transmissions in a 100 Mbit LAN.	29
3.1	Symmetric vs. asymmetric key cryptography.	37
3.2	Bandwidth division during counter-flooding under different conditions.	48
3.3	Effect of Ethernet flow control on TCP throughput under a DoS flooding attack.	49
4.1	Benchmark: verifying and solving modular square root puzzles on Intel Core 2 Quad Q9400 2.66 GHz.	66
5.1	Benchmark: throughput of cryptographic hash functions on Intel Core 2 Quad Q9400 2.66 GHz (one core active).	80
6.1	Performance comparison of the modular squaring operation on different platforms.	107
6.2	Computation time of $r = 2^t \bmod \varphi(n)$ on an Intel Core 2 Duo E6750 2.66 GHz for different puzzle difficulties $t = T \cdot S$ with an Intel Core 2 Duo T9900 3.06 GHz as reference machine for S.	108

List of Tables

List of Abbreviations

ADSL	Asymmetric Digital Subscriber Line
AES	Advanced Encryption Standard
ARP	Address Resolution Protocol
CBC	Cipher Block Chaining
CLL	Cryptographic Link Layer
DDoS	Distributed Denial-of-Service
DHCP	Dynamic Host Configuration Protocol
DNS	Domain Name System
DoS	Denial-of-Service
DSA	Digital Signature Algorithm
FPGA	Field-Programmable Gate Array
GPU	Graphics Processing Unit
GUI	Graphical User Interface
HMAC	Hashed Message Authentication Code
HTTP	Hypertext Transfer Protocol
HTTPS	Hypertext Transfer Protocol Secure
ICMP	Internet Control Message Protocol
IDS	Intrusion Detection System
IP	Internet Protocol
ISP	Internet Service Provider
IV	Initialization Vector
LAN	Local Area Network
MAC	Media Access Control
MiM	Man in the Middle
MTU	Maximum Transmission Unit

List of Abbreviations

NIC	Network Interface Controller
NTP	Network Time Protocol
OSRTLP	Offline Submission with RSA Time-Lock Puzzles
PKI	Public Key Infrastructure
RSA	Ron Rivest, Adi Shamir, and Leonard Adleman
RTT	Round-Trip Time
SA	Security Association
SSH	Secure Shell
SSL	Secure Sockets Layer
TCP	Transmission Control Protocol
TLS	Transport Layer Security
TTL	Time To Live
UDP	User Datagram Protocol
UMTS	Universal Mobile Telecommunications System
WPA	Wi-Fi Protected Access

Chapter 1

Introduction

Denial of-Service (DoS) attacks pose one of the major threats to Web services on the Internet and have become a common means of cyber warfare. In the most common scenario, an attacker, or in case of a *distributed Denial-of-Service (DDoS)* attack a group of attacking systems, tries to exhaust the resources (CPU time, memory, or disk space) of a server by overwhelming it with a flood of bogus requests. The aim is to slow down and finally to overload the server so that it cannot respond to legitimate clients anymore and the service provided becomes unavailable. But a network resource can be also rendered unusable by exploiting vulnerabilities of the underlying protocol, e. g., through disruption of configuration or state information. In this case the injection of a few specially crafted packets may be sufficient for a DoS attack to succeed. DoS attacks are mounted to pursue different goals—they may be politically or economically motivated, some attackers just aim at demonstrating their power while others are driven by revenge or try to extort their victim. A report on DDoS attacks in the second half of 2011 [GN12] presents current numbers and gives a rough picture of their impact on politics and business.

However, DoS attacks affect not only Internet services. They are also conducted in corporate Intranets and *Local Area Networks (LANs)* to disrupt communication within a single entity. Especially public LANs like Wi-Fi hotspots pose promising targets for an effective DoS attack. In this thesis, we put our focus on how to secure a local area network against DoS and how to prevent a number of other attacks that result from missing authentication mechanisms between the link and the network layer. The main vulnerability in wired and wireless LANs is the lack of initial address authenticity. An

Chapter 1 Introduction

attacker can easily take on different identities and emit packets bearing a foreign or a fake sender address. In contrast, forging the sender address in the Internet without the packet getting dropped by intermediate routers is far more complicated. Filtering mechanisms that can recognize a flood of requests in the Internet based on their origin do not work in LANs. DoS countermeasures developed to mitigate attacks carried out over the Internet turn out to have drawbacks when being applied in LANs. Thus, safeguarding LAN communication constitutes a challenging and relevant issue.

Our attack model assumes an adversary (or a group of them) that is powerful but not omnipotent. Basically, we suppose that the attacker can eavesdrop on the traffic, can inject packets with arbitrary contents and especially manipulate all protocol headers including the sender address. But modifying foreign packets and destroying them in switches or in the medium to a significant extent is beyond his capabilities. Being equipped with bandwidth, processors, and memory our adversary mainly performs software-based attacks on the protocol level and this is the starting point for us to counteract. Active hardware-based attacks utilizing special devices are beyond the scope of this work.

The vision is to make communication in local area networks secure and DoS-resistant. Our contribution to it consists of two main building blocks: First, provide a comprehensive security protocol that ensures authentication and confidentiality between neighboring hosts from the link layer upwards. This involves the use of public-key cryptography which is quite costly compared to symmetric-key algorithms. Second, develop new and improve existing techniques to safeguard security protocols relying on public-key cryptography (and in general protocols that involve processing of complex requests) against DoS attacks. The two DoS countermeasures presented in this thesis—one deals with sending packets, the other with solving puzzles—share a common principle of defense. In case of a DoS attack the hosts requesting service from the victimized machine have to pay for it using some currency, e.g., bandwidth or CPU cycles, and the more they pay, the higher will be their chances to get service and the lower will be the impact of the attack.

Using puzzles to mitigate DoS attacks is a known approach in the literature. We show that existing puzzle schemes cannot be safely used in LANs since they are vulnerable to counterattacks. Hence, we develop a new DoS protection scheme based on controlled flooding of packets. Then we revisit the puzzle approach and introduce a novel puzzle construction that offers some advantages over existing schemes. Our construction is generic, i.e., its application is not limited to LANs. Next, we present an elaborate puzzle architecture that is specifically tailored to the attack potential in LANs and can benefit from the new puzzle construction. Finally, we pursue the idea of cryptographic puzzles and propose a puzzle scheme derived from the RSA public-key cryptosystem that can be used for a very different purpose than DoS protection, namely for offline submission of documents.

The feasibility of the approaches introduced in this work is supported either by a fully working implementation or at least by prototypes and real-world measurements. Our protocols, algorithms, and schemes are naturally based on many previous works in different areas of cryptography, DoS protection, and networking. We therefore discuss related work in each chapter separately.

In Chapter 2, we introduce our first major contribution, the *Cryptographic Link Layer (CLL)*, which is a layer 2/3 security extension for LANs. Ethernet and IP form the basis of the vast majority of LAN installations. But these protocols do not provide comprehensive security mechanisms, and thus give way for a plethora of attack scenarios. CLL provides authentication and confidentiality to the hosts in the LAN by safeguarding all layer 2 traffic including ARP and DHCP handshakes. It is transparent to existing protocol implementations, especially to the ARP module and to DHCP clients and servers. Beyond fending off external attackers, CLL also protects from malicious behavior of authenticated clients. We discuss the CLL protocol, motivate the underlying design decisions, and finally present implementations of CLL for both Windows and Linux. Their performance is demonstrated through real-world evaluation and benchmarking.

CLL, as well as the majority of security protocols, employs public-key cryptography for authentication in the connection setup phase. However, verification of digital signatures is an expensive task compared to symmetric-key operations and may become the target for DoS attacks where the adversary floods the victim host with fake signature packets trying to overload it. In Chapter 3, we present *counter-flooding*, a new defense mechanism against DoS attacks on public-key handshakes in LANs that exploit the lack of

Chapter 1 Introduction

initial address authenticity. A benign host having a signature packet addressed to a host which is currently under attack ensures the processing of its packet by flooding copies of this packet for a short period of time itself. The key idea is for the victim host to verify only a fixed number of signatures per time period without becoming overloaded and to select those packets for verification that have the largest number of duplicates. Under weak assumptions we prove that the packet from the benign host will be among them. We derive bounds for our counter-flooding mechanism to succeed and perform experiments with Ethernet switches to study the bandwidth division between concurrent flows under overload conditions.

A prominent countermeasure against DoS attacks which is known in the literature for more than a decade now are *client puzzles*. The victimized server demands from the clients to commit computing resources before it processes their requests. To get service, a client must solve a cryptographic puzzle and submit the right solution. However, existing client puzzle schemes have some drawbacks. They are either parallelizable, coarse-grained or can be used only interactively. In Chapter 4, we thus introduce a novel scheme for client puzzles which relies on the computation of square roots modulo a prime. *Modular square root puzzles* are non-parallelizable, i.e., the solution cannot be obtained faster than scheduled by distributing the puzzle to multiple machines or CPU cores, and they can be employed both interactively and non-interactively. Our puzzles provide polynomial granularity and compact solution and verification functions. Benchmark results demonstrate the feasibility of our approach to mitigate DoS attacks on hosts in 1 or even 10 Gbit networks. In addition, we show how to raise the efficiency of our puzzle scheme by introducing a bandwidth-based cost factor for the client.

Most existing client puzzle schemes are interactive. Upon receiving a request the server constructs a puzzle and asks the client to solve this challenge before processing its request. But the packet with the puzzle parameters sent from server to client lacks authentication. Especially in LANs the attacker might mount a counterattack on the clients by injecting faked packets with bogus puzzle parameters bearing the server's sender address. A client receiving a plethora of bogus challenges may become overloaded and probably will not be able to solve the genuine challenge issued by the authentic server. Thus, its request remains unanswered. Non-interactive client puzzles, on the other hand, enable the attacker to gain more power by precomputing solutions. Chapter 5 presents a *secure client puzzle architecture* which overcomes the described authentication issue and prevents the precomputation of puzzle solutions. In our architecture client puzzles, e.g., the modular square root puzzles introduced in the previous chapter, are employed non-interactively and constructed by the client from a periodically changing, secure *random beacon*. A special beacon server broadcasts beacon messages that can be easily verified by matching their hash values against a list of beacon fingerprints which has been obtained in advance. We develop sophisticated techniques to provide a robust beacon service. This involves synchronization aspects and especially the secure deployment of beacon fingerprints.

In Chapter 6, we look at a very different application area for puzzles in the context of timed-release cryptography. We propose a non-interactive *RSA time-lock puzzle* scheme whose level of difficulty can be arbitrarily chosen by artificially enlarging the public exponent. Solving a puzzle for a message m means for Bob to encrypt m with Alice's public puzzle key by repeated modular squaring. The number of squarings to perform determines the puzzle complexity. This puzzle is non-parallelizable. Thus, the solution time cannot be shortened significantly by employing many machines and it varies only slightly across modern CPUs. Alice can quickly verify the puzzle solution by decrypting the ciphertext with a regular private key operation. The main application is an *offline submission protocol* which enables an author currently being offline to commit to his document before the deadline by continuously solving an RSA puzzle based on that document. After regaining Internet connectivity, he submits his document along with the puzzle solution which is a proof for the timely completion of the document. We have implemented a platform-independent tool performing all parts of our offline submission protocol: puzzle benchmark, issuing a time-lock RSA certificate, solving a puzzle and finally verifying the solution for a submitted document. Two other applications we propose for RSA time-lock puzzles are trial certificates and a CEO disclosing the signing private key to his deputy.

Finally, we conclude this thesis with a summary in Chapter 7 where we reflect the major contributions.

Chapter 1 Introduction

Chapter 2

CLL: A Cryptographic Link Layer for LANs

Ethernet and the Internet Protocol (IP) are the main building blocks for the vast majority of modern Local Area Networks (LANs). However, these protocols, and thus virtually all installed LANs, do not provide comprehensive security mechanisms. Hence, malicious local users are potentially able to eavesdrop, to inject or modify information, or to take on fake identities.

One especially critical component is the *Address Resolution Protocol (ARP)* [Plu82]. It performs the task of coupling the network layer with the link layer by resolving IP addresses into the corresponding MAC addresses. However, ARP lacks an authentication mechanism, making it vulnerable to different types of attacks. This constitutes a severe threat in every LAN that is accessible to not fully trustworthy users. By emitting ARP messages with wrong IP/MAC mappings—commonly referred to as *ARP spoofing*—a malicious user can *impersonate* other hosts, intercept and modify foreign IP traffic by becoming a *Man in the Middle (MiM)*, or mount a *Denial of Service (DoS)* attack against other hosts. Using freely available tools, e.g. [Mon, Ett], ARP spoofing can be easily performed even by users without deeper knowledge of the underlying protocols.

Preventing ARP attacks in the case of dynamic IP addresses requires to take also the *Dynamic Host Configuration Protocol (DHCP)* [Dro97] into account. It is employed in almost every LAN to automatically assign IP addresses and configuration parameters. It does not provide an authentication mechanism either and thus can also become the target of various attacks. By setting up a rogue DHCP server and announcing forged IP addresses for the default gateway or the DNS server, an adversary is able to run a MiM

Chapter 2 CLL: A Cryptographic Link Layer for LANs

or DoS attack against clients requesting an IP address via DHCP. Furthermore, the legitimate DHCP server is also vulnerable. In a *DHCP starvation attack* the adversary takes on many different client identities (usually MAC addresses) and requests each time a new IP address, until the server's address pool gets exhausted. Thereby the attacker can prevent new clients from acquiring a valid IP configuration.

Since modern operating systems enable the injection of raw Ethernet packets containing arbitrary MAC and IP addresses in their headers even in user mode, there exists no external barrier which would impede address fraud. The outlined attack scenarios are covered in more detail, e.g., in [AKO+04, BOR03, VP07].

In this chapter, we tackle the challenge of securing the communication in local area networks, including ARP and DHCP. We introduce a comprehensive layer 2/3 security protocol—the *Cryptographic Link Layer (CLL)*. It provides authentication and confidentiality between neighboring hosts in Ethernet LANs. Each machine gets identified by its IP/MAC address pair. Beyond safeguarding ARP and DHCP, CLL protects arbitrary layer 2 traffic, especially all encapsulated IP packets. A paper on CLL covering the central results of this chapter has been published in [JLSM08]. We propose to employ CLL, e.g., in enterprise and campus networks being often accessed by frequently changing, not fully trustworthy users as well as in all kinds of publicly accessible LANs (like Internet cafés or Wi-Fi hotspots). Note that CLL does not affect the operation of higher layer security protocols.

Beginning with an ARP request, CLL applies public-key cryptography to perform an initial handshake between two hosts with the aim to establish a security association. The two hosts prove their identity to each other and exchange keying material. Hereupon, secured IP data packets may be sent.

We have implemented and evaluated CLL on both Windows and Linux. In LANs running at 100 Mbit/s, our implementation operates at full wire-speed, thus securing the network without compromising the throughput. To ease the migration procedure, CLL-enabled machines can be configured to interoperate with ordinary, unsecured hosts. We make our CLL implementation available for free download including the sources, and complement it with a toolkit for key and certificate management [Jera].

The remainder of this chapter is organized as follows. In the next section, we review previous approaches to securing ARP, DHCP, and the link layer. Section 2.2 sketches the architecture of CLL, before Section 2.3 justifies the underlying cryptographic design decisions. In Sections 2.4 and 2.5, we detail the operation of CLL's protocol components. Section 2.6 describes the implementation of CLL and evaluates its performance. Finally, we conclude the chapter with a summary in Section 2.7.

2.1 Related Work

Above the link layer, there already exist well-proven security protocols which provide authentication and confidentiality by means of cryptography. *SSH* [YL06] and *SSL / TLS* [DR06] operate at the application level or directly below it. At the network layer, *IPsec* [KS05] can protect IP datagrams being exchanged between two end-points. However, IPsec does not authenticate the IP address of the communicating party. This enables an authorized IPsec user to impersonate the IP address of another host that is temporarily switched off or knocked out by a DoS attack. While SSH, SSL / TLS, and IPsec cannot protect from attacks on ARP and DHCP, the encryption performed by these protocols will still prevent the disclosure of sensitive data. An attacker would have to content himself with the power of rendering his victims unable to communicate.

Reviewing the attempts to cope with the insecurity of ARP, there exist two main directions. One is to detect the bulk of ARP attacks by means of a specialized Intrusion Detection System (IDS) like *Antidote* [Ant] or *ArpWatch* [Arp] and to warn the user or network administrator in time. Such tools monitor all incoming ARP messages and trigger an alarm, e.g., on observing an abnormally high number of ARP replies or a changed IP/MAC mapping. However, these ARP watchdogs cannot provide full protection against ARP attacks; in particular, they are not able to distinguish whether the MAC address in the first ARP reply is genuine or not. The other approach is to secure ARP by using cryptographic techniques. In the following, we discuss some current research taking this direction.

Gouda and Huang [GH03] specified a theoretical architecture with an ARP server sharing a symmetric key for message authentication with every host in the LAN. Each host

Chapter 2 CLL: A Cryptographic Link Layer for LANs

periodically notifies the server about its current IP/MAC mapping and resolves the MAC addresses of its neighbors with the aid of the ARP server. However, this does not prevent an authorized machine from purposely announcing a mapping of a neighboring host's IP address to its own MAC address. In contrast, CLL authenticates all hosts based on their IP/MAC address pair. It thus also avoids ARP spoofing attempts originating from malicious, but authorized users. Furthermore, CLL does not require a central server.

In [BOR03], Bruschi et al. introduced *Secure ARP (S-ARP)* which uses public-key signatures to authenticate the ARP replies. All hosts in the LAN hold a private/public key pair and initially enroll at a central server, the *Authoritative Key Distributor (AKD)*. The AKD maintains a repository of public keys and the corresponding (static) IP addresses. Whenever a host requires a neighbor's public key to verify the signature of an ARP reply, it inquires about it from the AKD. The AKD's reply packet is digitally signed as well and the AKD's public key is preinstalled on all machines. S-ARP comes with an implementation for Linux 2.4, but it requires a kernel patch and does not support dynamically assigned IP addresses.

On the basis of S-ARP, Lootah et al. proposed *Ticket-based ARP (TARP)* [LEM07]. It foregoes a central key server and instead employs digitally signed attestations of IP/MAC mappings, so-called *tickets*. The tickets are issued by a trusted party, the *Local Ticket Agent (LTA)*. The host responding to an ARP request attaches its ticket to the ARP reply and thereby proves the validity. Since the LTA's public key is preinstalled on each host, received tickets can be verified quickly. In comparison to S-ARP, TARP requires at most one public-key operation per ARP exchange and no private key operations, and thus offers better performance. However, the authors state that an attacker is able to impersonate a host that is currently offline, by replaying its previously captured ticket. TARP has been implemented on Linux 2.6 with support for DHCP-assigned IP addresses. Note, however, that both S-ARP and TARP aim to secure only ARP, while CLL provides overall layer 2 security by safeguarding DHCP and data packets as well.

RFC 3118 [DA01] specifies how DHCP can be extended by an authentication mechanism. In this scheme, the DHCP server shares with each client a symmetric key. It is used to authenticate the DHCP messages. However, DHCPDISCOVER, the first message sent by the client, remains unauthenticated. Consequently, users still might be able to perform a DHCP starvation attack. This is not the case with CLL. Another drawback is that currently no DHCP implementations with RFC 3118 support are available.

Applying cryptography at the link layer is common in Wi-Fi networks. *Wi-Fi Protected Access (WPA)* and *WPA2 (IEEE 802.11i)* provide authentication and confidentiality between wireless nodes and the access point. The IEEE working group 802.1AE [IEE] specifies *MACsec* as the analog of WPA/WPA2 for LANs. In contrast to CLL, WPA/WPA2 and MACsec authenticate hosts based only on their MAC address. The content of ARP and DHCP control packets encapsulated in layer 2 frames is not examined. Therefore these protocols cannot protect from ARP and DHCP attacks originating from legitimate users. Moreover, we are not aware of any MACsec implementation being available at this time.

The main contribution of this chapter is a novel, comprehensive approach to layer 2 security, which provides a more complete protection of the LAN than even a combination of three existing protocols (e. g., TARP, RFC 3118, and IPsec) could achieve. That is because besides eliminating the discussed shortcomings of these protocols, CLL also authenticates broadcast traffic. The tackled security problems are all related to each other—they arise from the lack of authentication at layer 2 and the link to layer 3. Thus, a comprehensive approach to solve them seems appropriate.

2.2 Protocol Overview

CLL is designed as a transparent filtering service between the network adapter and the IP stack. It thus operates at the border between the link and the network layer, as displayed in Figure 2.1. All outgoing packets including the Ethernet header are authenticated and their payload is optionally encrypted before they are handed over to the network card for transmission. Incoming packets are passed to the IP stack only after they have been successfully authenticated and—if applicable—decrypted. CLL can be enabled or disabled without modifying the other protocol stack components. For them, CLL's services are transparent. But in fact, CLL appends its cryptographic headers to outgoing packets, and puts its own ID into the EtherType field of the Ethernet header.

Chapter 2 CLL: A Cryptographic Link Layer for LANs

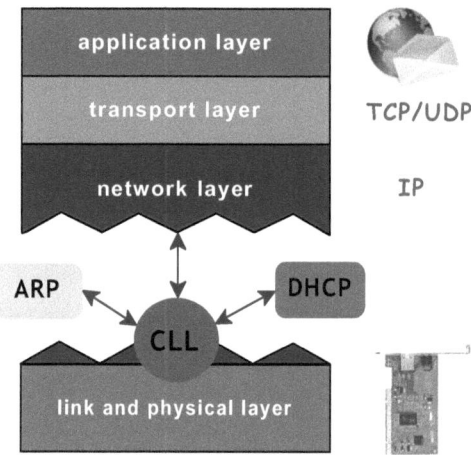

Figure 2.1: CLL in the protocol stack.

From successfully authenticated incoming packets CLL strips off its cryptographic headers and restores the original EtherType value before passing them up. While the operation of CLL does not require any modifications to switches, routers must either support CLL (and benefit from it) or exchange packets with the end systems in the standard, insecure manner.

CLL identifies hosts by their IP/MAC address pair. Each machine on the LAN holds a private/public key pair and a certificate issued by the local Certificate Authority (CA)—usually the network administrator—which establishes the binding between its public key, the MAC and the IP address. To verify certificates, each host requires the CA's public key. Typically it will be installed in the form of a self-signed certificate along with the host's own certificate, but a more complex Public Key Infrastructure (PKI) to support multiple LANs is also conceivable.

Basically, CLL divides all network traffic into four packet types: *ARP* and *DHCP*[1] control packets, *unicast* and *broadcast IP* data packets. Authentication is performed for

---
[1]Though being encapsulated in an UDP segment and an IP datagram, we handle DHCP messages as a separate layer 3 packet type due to the functional position of DHCP below the network layer.

2.2 Protocol Overview

all packet types and, in addition, an optional payload encryption is provided for unicast IP packets.

While ARP and broadcast IP packets are authenticated by means of public-key cryptography (digital signatures in conjunction with certificates), unicast IP and DHCP packets get secured using fast symmetric key algorithms. Safeguarding unicast IP packets with a message authentication code and optionally a block cipher requires each pair of communicating hosts to share a secret key. For that purpose, CLL employs a key exchange protocol to negotiate shared keys on-demand. Since the IP traffic flow between two hosts always begins with an ARP exchange, CLL adopts it to establish a *security association (SA)* between the two peers. The two machines authenticate each other, negotiate a secret key and agree on the cryptographic algorithms to protect their IP packets. The establishment of an SA is subsequently referred to as *handshake*.

To determine the sender's (claimed) identity during the authentication of incoming packets, CLL examines the Ethernet header and, depending on the protocol, also the ARP, IP, or DHCP header. Where applicable, it performs a consistency check: the sender's MAC address can be also found in the ARP header or—in case of a DHCP client—in the DHCP header, and it must match the address specified in the Ethernet header. Such a cross-layer consistency check is not performed by other protocol layers. It is, however, crucially important to ward off ARP spoofing and DHCP starvation attacks. Layer 2 authentication alone would not suffice for this purpose.

The following listing summarizes the various LAN attacks fended off by CLL:

- *ARP spoofing:* impersonation, MiM and DoS attack

- *DHCP spoofing:* rogue DHCP server (MiM & DoS), DHCP starvation attack (DoS)

- *generic unicast attacks:* injection of spoofed packets, eavesdropping

- *generic broadcast attacks:* injection of spoofed packets, special case: smurf attack[2].

---

[2]Flooding the victim via spoofed broadcast ping messages being answered by all other hosts.

2.3 Cryptographic Design Decisions

The security philosophy of CLL is to provide the user with a suite of up-to-date cryptographic algorithms and corresponding parameters, letting her choose between them on her own responsibility. Such a design has the advantage of considering individual security perceptions, allowing to trade off between highest-level security and best performance, and supporting the prompt exchange of an algorithm being reported as broken. With our implementation, we nevertheless provide a reasonable default configuration to assist users without deeper understanding of cryptography. The general level of protection provided by CLL may be also selected. Either CLL just authenticates all types of packets or it additionally also encrypts the payload of unicast IP packets (including the IP header). Skipping the encryption step will result in a better performance and should be done whenever a higher layer security protocol like IPsec already ensures confidentiality. CLL allows to use different ciphers and hash functions in each direction of an SA. With regard to system complexity, we however prescribe the algorithms used for key exchange, key derivation, and DHCP packet authentication. Table 2.1 summarizes the algorithms proposed for CLL and supported by our implementation.

During the handshake CLL applies the Diffie-Hellman [DH76] key agreement protocol to exchange a symmetric *master key* with perfect forward secrecy between the two peers. Since handshake packets are digitally signed, there exists no susceptibility to man-in-the-middle attacks. To the negotiated master key we apply a deterministic key derivation function to generate for each direction two properly sized keys—one for the message authentication code and one for the optional cipher.

CLL guarantees the authenticity of unicast IP and DHCP packets by means of a *Hashed Message Authentication Code (HMAC)* [BCK96] attached to the end of each packet. In addition to authentication, CLL offers to protect unicast IP packets from eavesdropping by optionally encrypting them with a block cipher in *Cipher Block Chaining (CBC)* mode. When establishing an SA, we generate a random *Initialization Vector (IV)* and use afterwards the last encrypted block of the preceding packet as the next packet's IV. Since transmissions on the link layer are unreliable, the sender also prepends the current IV to each packet. If the payload size is not a multiple of the block size, random padding bytes are appended. We first encrypt the plaintext and then compute the HMAC for

Table 2.1: Algorithms and parameters in CLL.

message auth. codes	• HMAC with MD5, SHA-160/256, RIPEMD-160 or HAS-160 • 128 – 256 bit key length
encryption	• optionally with a block cipher in CBC mode, 128 – 256 bit key length • available ciphers: Twofish, AES, RC6, RC5, Blowfish, MARS, Serpent, CAST-128/256, SEED, GOST
key exchange	Diffie-Hellman, 2048-bit group No. 14 from the IPsec specification
key derivation	IEEE 1363a Key Derivation Function 2 (KDF2) using RIPEMD-160
key rollover	periodically on demand, e. g., every 30 min
digital signatures	• RSA with variable key length (typically 1024 – 2048 bits) • RSASSA-PSS signature scheme with SHA-160/256 or RIPEMD-160
certificates	X.509 v3 with RSA signature, ASN.1 BER/DER encoding

the ciphertext, since this is the only order that is generally considered secure [Kra01]. It also enables to detect a forged packet without the need to decrypt it.

To sign handshake and broadcast IP packets, CLL applies the well-known RSA algorithm [RSA78] along with certificates. RSA offers the great advantage of supporting public-key signatures and encryption with a single key pair. And though CLL's security architecture does not require any public-key encryption, in practice the local CA can make use of RSA encryption to securely deploy the DHCP HMAC keys to the users.

2.4 Operation of CLL in Detail

2.4.1 Basic Packet Format

When securing Ethernet frames, CLL inserts its own headers and replaces the EtherType value in the Ethernet header with its own identifier (0x07D0, otherwise unassigned by IEEE). Figure 2.2 depicts the generic layout of an Ethernet frame safeguarded by CLL.

Chapter 2 CLL: A Cryptographic Link Layer for LANs

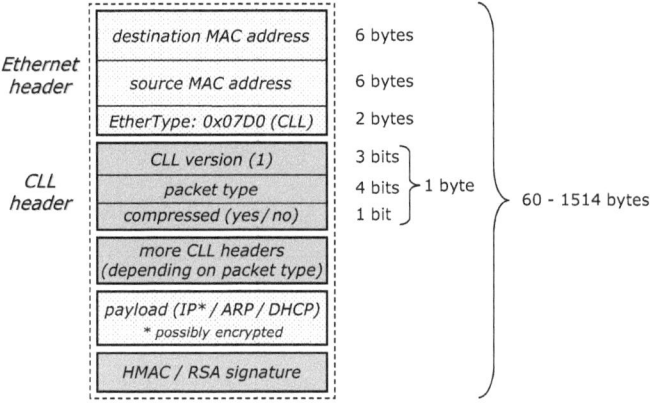

Figure 2.2: An Ethernet frame in CLL.

The *CLL header* is placed behind the Ethernet header. It has been designed as a compact bit field to save overhead. It consists of a version number (currently 1) like in IP, a field specifying the encapsulated packet type (*unicast* or *broadcast IP packet*, *ARP handshake packet*, *DHCP client* or *server packet*, internal *certificate packet*), and a boolean flag stating whether the payload has been optionally compressed by CLL. This main CLL header is followed by one or more inner headers depending on the encapsulated packet's type. Therein we store, among cryptographic parameters, the original EtherType number. Behind the inner headers resides the payload, i.e., an ARP, IP, or DHCP packet. Finally, each secured Ethernet frame terminates with an authentication field containing either an HMAC (unicast IP and DHCP packets) or an RSA signature (ARP handshake and broadcast IP packets) computed over the whole frame.

2.4.2 ARP Handshake and SA Setup

Overview

To safeguard unicast IP packets, CLL needs to establish an SA between each pair of communicating hosts. For this, CLL takes advantage of the ARP mechanism and expands

2.4 Operation of CLL in Detail

it at the same time with authentication. Figure 2.3 illustrates this ARP handshake between two hosts A and B.

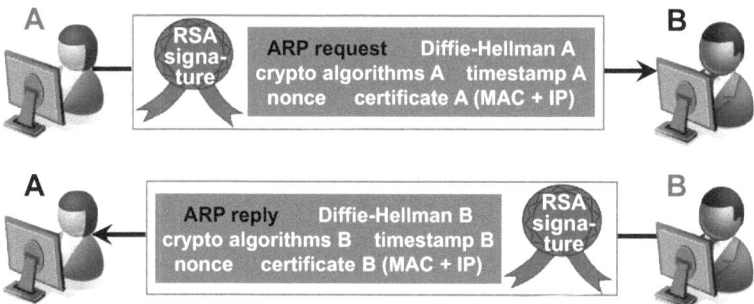

Figure 2.3: ARP handshake: Diffie-Hellman key exchange in conjunction with RSA signatures.

When started, a CLL implementation should first flush the ARP cache, thus ensuring that all IP traffic to other hosts is preceded by an ARP request. Having intercepted the ARP request, CLL wraps it up into a digitally signed handshake packet. It includes the host certificate and cryptographic parameters to establish the SA. The handshake packet is broadcasted like an ordinary ARP request and every station on the LAN checks whether it holds the inquired IP address. At the destination host, CLL verifies the certificate of the requesting host and validates the packet's signature. Invalid packets are dropped. Then it must be checked whether the sender's IP/MAC address pair claimed in the ARP request (and its MAC address stated in the Ethernet header) matches the one specified in its certificate.

If the handshake packet turns out to be valid, CLL creates a new SA with the requesting host, based on the local and the received cryptographic parameters. Finally, CLL strips off everything from the handshake packet except for the ARP header, restores the ARP EtherType number in the Ethernet header and passes the resulting ordinary ARP request up the protocol stack to the ARP module. The ARP module creates then an ARP table entry for the requesting host, and responds with an ARP reply. This reply gets intercepted again and is encapsulated into a digitally signed handshake packet analogously to the ARP request, along with the local cryptographic parameters and the

Chapter 2 CLL: A Cryptographic Link Layer for LANs

host certificate. CLL then unicasts this second handshake packet to the requesting host like a usual ARP reply. In the following, we refer to the first handshake packet as the *handshake request* and to the second one as the *handshake reply*. On the requesting host the handshake reply undergoes the same verification process before the SA is established and the ARP reply is passed up to the ARP module.

Creating an SA implies the computation of a joint master key from the public and private Diffie-Hellman values. From the master key, CLL then derives the four keys for the HMAC and the optional block cipher. At any time, only one SA is permitted per host pair.

Handshake Packet Details

We employ a UNIX timestamp and a nonce to protect against replay attacks. CLL requires the clocks of all hosts on the LAN to be synchronized within reasonable limits decided on by the network administrator, e.g., in the range of 2–5 minutes. This can be easily achieved if the users manually adjust their computer's clock occasionally. An automatic clock synchronization, for instance by using NTP [Mil92], is also possible after having established an SA to a trustworthy server.

The nonce is a random 64-bit number generated by the initiator of the handshake, which expects to find it repeated in the handshake reply. It ensures that the peer actually participates in the protocol, i.e., its handshake reply has not been replayed. Due to the nonce, it is not necessary to verify the timestamp in the handshake reply. It must, however, be stored for comparisons with timestamps of possibly future handshake requests.

The other important handshake element are the cryptographic parameters. Each host specifies the hash function configured for the HMAC and the block cipher potentially chosen to protect the payload against eavesdropping, along with the key sizes. A compression algorithm may be specified as well, if a host intends to compress its outgoing unicast IP packets. Moreover, each party states how long the SA should be valid before it is either extended or removed due to inactivity. The actual SA validity period is the minimum of the two claims. However, it may not fall below a threshold currently set to 15 minutes to prevent permanent handshakes or renegotiations.

Retransmissions and Conflicts

CLL addresses the possibility of a handshake packet loss by means of retransmissions. In case of a lost (or just unanswered) handshake request the standard ARP retransmission mechanism will trigger a new ARP request. Having intercepted this ARP request, CLL retransmits the respective cached handshake request after updating its timestamp and signature. Through caching we avoid the computation-intensive generation of new Diffie-Hellman values.

The loss of a handshake reply will also result in a retransmission of the corresponding handshake request. The answering peer caches the received original handshake request as well as its own handshake reply. It is therefore able to recognize the incoming duplicate handshake request, and retransmits its handshake reply. Due to the receiver relying on the nonce, we can even omit to update timestamp and signature in this case.

Theoretically, it is conceivable that two hosts without an SA concurrently send each other a handshake request, when both of them have a pending IP datagram destined for the other one. However, only the creation of a single SA is allowed between two hosts. CLL resolves this issue by performing an integer comparison between the two 48-bit MAC addresses: the handshake request of the host with the higher MAC address "wins".

Complete and Incomplete SAs

From the point of view of a host, we refer to an SA as *complete* when it is known for sure that the peer has also established the SA. Host A as the initiator of an ARP handshake can set up the SA with its peer B only after having received the handshake reply. A's SA is therefore complete right from the start. Host A can immediately send secured unicast IP packets to its peer B and be certain that B will be able to verify and decrypt them.

In contrast, host B first has an *incomplete* SA, as long as it cannot be sure whether A has received its handshake reply. Usually, the IP datagram of host A that triggered the ARP request will quickly reach host B and thereby confirm the set up SA. However, as long as this is not the case, host B may not transmit any IP packets to its peer—A might not be able to authenticate them. Instead, in the unlikely case that B wants to transmit to A before A has sent the first packet, B must queue its IP datagram and send a new handshake request to A. This enforces the creation of a new SA, replacing the existing incomplete one.

Safeguarding against Replay Attacks

While the initiator of the SA protects itself against a replayed handshake reply with the aid of a nonce, its peer has to rely on the timestamp check when judging the freshness of an incoming handshake request. However, a timestamp is considered valid within a period of several minutes (smaller than the minimum SA duration) to tolerate time deviations. It hence does not assure a complete protection by itself. An attacker may try to replace an existing SA by replaying a captured outdated handshake request bearing a timestamp which is still valid. CLL fends off such attacks by comparing the timestamp of a new handshake request with the timestamp of the handshake request or reply which led to the establishment of the currently existing SA. The use of timestamps avoids the necessity of a third message for a second nonce in the other direction, which would render the ARP handshake more complex.

2.4.3 Unicast IP Packets

Having created ARP table entries and established an SA, unicast IP packets can be transmitted between the two peers. This is illustrated in Figure 2.4. While host A encrypts its packets with the block cipher AES and authenticates them with an HMAC using the hash function SHA-1, its peer B employs Twofish and MD5. Taking the sender's MAC address the receiver looks up the corresponding SA to verify the packet's HMAC, sequence number, source IP address, and to decrypt the IP datagram. Only if the peer is a router, its IP address may differ from the source address stated in the IP header.

2.4 Operation of CLL in Detail

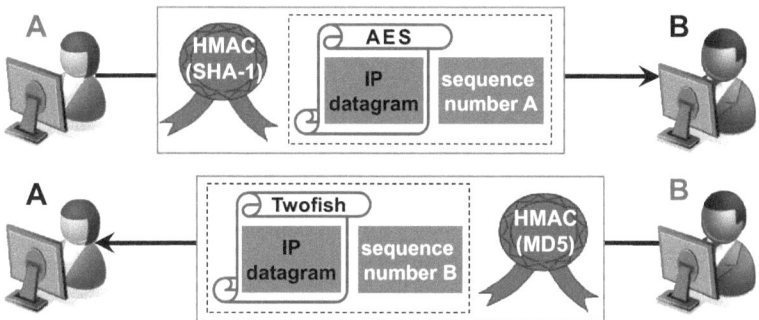

Figure 2.4: Transmission of unicast IP packets safeguarded with a block cipher and a message authentication code.

Each unicast IP packet contains a sequence number to protect against replay attacks. It is incremented by one with each packet sent to the respective destination. The receiver tolerates packet losses and only checks whether a packet's sequence number is larger than that of its predecessor. The sequence numbers are transmitted as plaintext to avoid an unnecessary decryption of replayed unicast IP packets. However, in order not to reveal the number of packets exchanged between two hosts so far, we generate the initial sequence numbers—one for each direction—at random.

Note that once having created an SA, CLL can also secure unicast packets carrying some other layer 3 protocol, e. g., Novell's IPX.

2.4.4 Periodical Key Rollover

By design, an SA has a short lifetime of typically 15–60 minutes like an ARP cache entry. But if any IP packets are transmitted during this period, it is renewed by a new Diffie-Hellman key exchange. New session keys for the HMAC and block cipher as well as sequence numbers are derived from a new master key. We call the extension of an SA *renegotiation*. Figure 2.5 illustrates the messages exchanged between two peers to extend their SA.

Chapter 2 CLL: A Cryptographic Link Layer for LANs

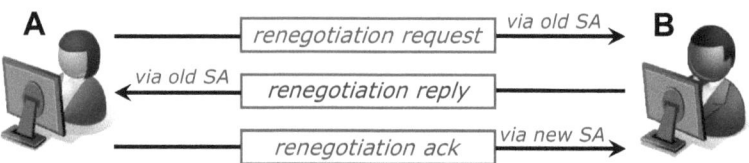

Figure 2.5: Renegotiation—renewing an SA.

The *renegotiation request* and *reply* are the counterparts of the handshake request and reply. They are transferred through the existing SA like usual unicast packets. Each peer establishes a new SA after receiving the corresponding renegotiation packet. Just like when initially setting up an SA, host A's SA is complete from the beginning on, while host B first has an incomplete SA. But in case of a renegotiation, we cannot expect that an IP packet will be transmitted from A to B shortly and render B's SA complete as well. Therefore, host A has to explicitly acknowledge the reception of the renegotiation reply. It does so by means of a *renegotiation ack* sent through the new SA.

The renegotiation is initiated by the peer that first determines the expiration of the SA according to its clock. Concurrent renegotiation attempts are resolved in the same way as in the ARP handshake by performing a MAC address comparison.

During the renegotiation the peers re-exchange and re-validate their *current* certificates to address a possible expiration of the previous ones, especially in case of short-lived certificates issued via DHCP. While a renegotiation is in progress, pending IP packets destined for the peer can be still transferred through the old SA, i.e., there is no need to delay and queue them. We address the possibility of renegotiation packet losses by means of a retransmission mechanism.

2.4.5 Broadcast Packets

CLL authenticates broadcast IP packets like handshake packets by means of an RSA signature. To verify the signature, the receivers require the sender's host certificate. However, the variable payload size of a broadcast packet may well be too large to piggyback the certificate and still stay within the maximum segment size limit. Therefore, we broadcast the certificate in advance in a special *certificate packet*. CLL sends a certificate packet only when dispatching a broadcast packet and when more than a minute has passed since the previous certificate transmission, i.e., periodically on demand. All hosts on the LAN cache the received host certificates. Thus they need to validate each certificate only once and henceforth have the correct public key readily available for future signature verifications.

Like handshake packets, broadcast packets are protected against replay attacks by means of a timestamp combined with an additional counter. If a host sends more than one broadcast packet at the same UNIX time (i.e., within one second), it increments this counter with each packet by one. All receivers store for each sender the timestamp and counter from its last broadcast packet. Subsequent packets from the same sender must bear a newer timestamp or the same timestamp with a higher counter value.

When dealing with high-rate broadcast traffic, the generation of RSA signatures on a per-packet basis may become computationally infeasible in real-time. However, in this case it is conceivable to queue outgoing broadcast packets for a short time and sign the accumulated group of packets as a whole with a single private key operation before dispatching them. The receivers would reassemble this group and verify the overall signature attached to the last packet. A sophisticated but also more complex approach tolerating packet losses might be the application of a specialized broadcast authentication protocol like TESLA [PCTS02].

2.5 Integrating and Securing DHCP

2.5.1 Basic Concept

So far, we have described the case of a static IP configuration, where the local CA creates for each machine a *host certificate* incorporating its MAC and IP address. However, CLL also supports the automatic assignment of IP addresses by means of DHCP. The DHCP message exchange is safeguarded and extended. CLL protects DHCP not only from unauthorized attackers, but also from malicious behavior originating from authenticated hosts.

Chapter 2 CLL: A Cryptographic Link Layer for LANs

In case DHCP is used, the local CA issues a *base certificate* for each host, bearing only the machine's MAC address and no IP address. The DHCP server uses the base certificate as a template to generate a full-fledged host certificate, which contains the assigned IP address. Thus, it acts as a second CA. The host certificate issued by the DHCP server has the same validity period as the IP address lease. When extending the DHCP lease, the host certificate is renewed accordingly.

Securing DHCP implies the authentication of all DHCP packets and a consistency check of the DHCP header in client-originated messages. Since CLL supervises the complete DHCP traffic in a transparent way, it also takes on the automatic application for a host certificate and its issuing. Its operation does not require any modifications on the employed DHCP client or server. On the client side, CLL attaches the base certificate to the DHCPREQUEST message. On the server CLL verifies this request and strips off its own headers, before passing it up to the DHCP module. It then waits for the outgoing DHCPACK message. This message constitutes the confirmation that the DHCP server has assigned the requested IP address. CLL extracts from it the allocated IP address along with the lease time, and issues a corresponding host certificate. Piggybacked on the DHCPACK message, the new host certificate finally reaches the client, which can now finalize its IP configuration and is ready to establish SAs.

2.5.2 Authenticating the Packets

We have designed the authentication of DHCP packets in a way that allows to employ an HMAC from the beginning, without requiring an initial public-key handshake. DHCP traffic occurs only between the clients and typically one single trusted server controlled by the local CA. Therefore, the number of communicating host pairs is limited and it is feasible to statically configure pre-shared HMAC keys. This task may be performed during the certificate enrollment without any additional effort. The local CA can generate a secret HMAC key for a host along with its base certificate. After encrypting the HMAC key with the host's public RSA key it can deliver these items to the user, e.g., via e-mail.

If the issued HMAC key were completely random, one would have to promptly configure it on the DHCP server as well, which involves some effort. Instead, we use a single *DHCP*

2.5 Integrating and Securing DHCP

master key, a concept adopted from [DA01]. From this master key we derive for each host the corresponding HMAC key by means of a key derivation function. The master key is known only to the local CA and the DHCP server. The pair <*MAC address, expiration time of the base certificate*>, in the following denoted as *client ID*, serves as the derivation parameter. This scheme does not require to inform the DHCP server about any newly certified hosts.

Since all hosts include their client ID into every sent DHCP packet, the DHCP server can deduce the corresponding HMAC key in an ad-hoc fashion and authenticate the packet. Conversely, when the DHCP server responds to the client, it has the right HMAC key already available. By incorporating the expiration time of the base certificate into the client ID we restrict the lifetime of the HMAC key. DHCP packets with expired client IDs are thus easily dropped without further verification. This allows, for instance, to immediately ignore DHCPDISCOVER messages sent by no longer authorized hosts.

To protect against replay attacks, we employ the same technique already introduced with broadcast packets, i.e., a UNIX timestamp in conjunction with a counter for packets bearing the same timestamp. A consistency check of the MAC and IP addresses stated in the DHCP header renders the authentication complete.

2.5.3 Further Security Measures

We consider the two DHCP messages DHCPDECLINE and DHCPRELEASE as a security risk. The first one allows a malicious client to spuriously tell the DHCP server that the IP address assigned to it is already in use by some other machine, thus making a DHCP starvation attack possible. The second one is utilized to release an assigned IP address to the DHCP server's address pool before the corresponding lease has expired. However, we cannot force a host to give up its certificate, and a malicious user might continue to use its certificate and with it the released IP address, while the address has also been assigned to some other machine. Therefore, we decided to simply drop these messages. Note that this does not violate the DHCP specification: these messages are transmitted in an unreliable manner without any retransmissions, i.e., they may get lost en route anyway. Moreover, no host is obliged to release its IP address ahead of time.

CLL allows to restrict the number of authenticated DHCP packets originated by the same host that the DHCP server will process during a specified time interval. Thereby the server can be secured against overload caused by malicious or misconfigured clients, attempting to renew their IP address lease extremely often. This would force the server to continuously issue new host certificates, which includes an expensive private key operation.

These security measures prevent malicious behavior originating from authenticated hosts. Without them attacks on DHCP would be still feasible and one would have to extensively analyze the server's DHCP logfiles to backtrack the identity of the attacker.

2.6 Implementation and Evaluation

2.6.1 CLL as a Cross-Platform Service

We have implemented CLL in C++ as a *user-mode service* on both Windows (XP, 2003 Server, Vista, 7) and Linux (kernel 2.6) using Visual C++ 2008 and GNU GCC 4.x respectively. Our CLL implementation consists of a platform independent core, which interoperates with a tailored portability layer providing a consistent interface for OS specific functionality. The responsibilities of the portability layer include crafting and filtering raw Ethernet frames, configuring the network interface (ARP, IP, MTU), and the interfaces for threads and timers.

To set up a filter handler for Ethernet frames in user-mode, we employ the packet filtering framework *WinpkFilter* [Res] on Windows. On Linux, we have implemented a link layer filtering solution on our own. We unbind the real network adapter from the IP stack, transparently replace it with a virtual one (a tap device), and set up a raw PF_PACKET socket to send and receive Ethernet frames through the unbound real network adapter. A maybe somewhat more efficient kernel-level implementation of CLL's packet processing engine would constitute a complex and error-prone task, especially when targeting multiple platforms. We therefore leave it for future work. But despite the overhead of additional context switches, our user-mode approach achieves good performance, and is able to operate at wire-speed in 100 Mbit LANs. To support the large number of cryptographic algorithms proposed for CLL, we employ the comprehensive open source crypto library *Botan* [Llo].

Aiming to provide a real-world solution, we address in our implementation such issues like persistent storage of SA configurations (to tolerate an OS reboot) and backward compatibility. To support non-CLL capable devices like network printers or NAS and to enable a step-by-step migration, CLL can be configured to communicate with legacy hosts in the standard, insecure fashion. This is accomplished by providing the CLL-enabled hosts with a list of the legacy IP/MAC address pairs. CLL then sets up static ARP entries and thereby provides at least an unidirectional protection against ARP spoofing.

A toolkit assists users and network administrators in creating, signing, and managing certificates, generating keys, or benchmarking the available cryptographic algorithms. Since the drivers of common Wi-Fi adapters exhibit an Ethernet-compatible interface to the network stack, Wi-Fi networks can be secured by CLL as well. To demonstrate the general applicability of our protocol, we have even managed to port CLL to the Linksys WRT54G Wi-Fi router, which is equipped with a 200 MHz RISC processor, 16 MB RAM and 4 MB flash memory running on Linux 2.4.

2.6.2 Performance Evaluation

We have conducted a performance evaluation in a switched 100 Mbit LAN with two hosts A and B, where A is a laptop equipped with an AMD64 Turion 1.8 GHz CPU running Linux 2.6.20 (32-bit) and B is a PC with an Intel Core 2 Duo E6400 2.13 GHz processor running Windows XP SP-2. The presented results are averaged over multiple runs.

The first series of measurements, shown in Table 2.2, is devoted to the overhead of the ARP handshake. For digital signatures both hosts use an RSA-1024 module. By pinging the neighboring host with no previously established SA we measure the time to perform the ARP handshake and the subsequent ICMP echo exchange. We compare

Chapter 2 CLL: A Cryptographic Link Layer for LANs

Table 2.2: Performance of the ARP handshake.

action	duration in ms
1st ping $A \to B$ using CLL: ARP handshake	27.4
1st ping $A \to B$ without CLL: usual ARP exchange	0.92
generating the private & public DH value (2048 bits)	host A: 26.3 host B: 44.1
deriving the master key with DH	host A: 7.2 host B: 15.7
computing an RSA-1024 signature	host A: 3.1 host B: 5.7

it to the delay of the first ping in an ordinary unsecured setup, including a plain ARP message exchange.

Though it takes 30 times longer than a usual ARP exchange, the one-time delay of 27.4 ms induced by the ARP handshake with CLL is negligibly short for practical purposes. This low value is achieved due to an optimization in our implementation: we precompute the Diffie-Hellman values in a background thread, and thus have them readily available at the beginning of an ARP handshake. Otherwise the handshake would last $26.3 + 44.1 = 70.4$ ms longer. The delay of 27.4 ms can be broken down by measuring the computation time of the two dominating operations—the derivation of the master key with Diffie-Hellman and the creation of an RSA signature[3]. Deriving the master key is performed in parallel, thus taking $\max\{7.2, 15.7\} = 15.7$ ms, while signing is carried out sequentially and requires $3.1 + 5.7 = 8.8$ ms. Summing this up yields 24.5 ms. The remaining 2.9 ms are used for verification of the host certificates and handshake signatures, and also include the network round-trip time (RTT).

In the second series of measurements, we analyze the TCP throughput (using the tool *ttcp* [TTC]), the CPU load incurred at the sender and receiver, and the RTT between two hosts already sharing an SA. The results are shown in Table 2.3. When comparing the TCP throughput achievable with CLL to the result using a conventional, unsecured protocol stack, we observe only a very small decrease in speed of approximately 2 % without encryption and 3 % with encryption. It can be attributed quite exactly to the overhead induced by the additional CLL headers and fields. Encryption and authen-

---

[3]Though host B's CPU is faster than host A's CPU, the public-key operations are slowed down by missing big integer assembler optimizations in Botan on Windows platforms.

Table 2.3: Performance of unicast transmissions in a 100 Mbit LAN.

action	measured values	
TCP throughput using CLL:		
• HMAC(MD5)	A → B: 11 263 KB/s	55 / 26 % CPU (tx / rx)
	B → A: 11 312 KB/s	22 / 60 % CPU (tx / rx)
• Twofish / HMAC(MD5)	A → B: 11 113 KB/s	75 / 38 % CPU (tx / rx)
	B → A: 11 160 KB/s	31 / 76 % CPU (tx / rx)
TCP throughput without CLL	A → B: 11 522 KB/s	45 / 17 % CPU (tx / rx)
	B → A: 11 519 KB/s	10 / 44 % CPU (tx / rx)
RTT: 100 pings A → B using CLL	min: 0.287 ms ∅: 0.377 ms	max: 0.501 ms σ: 0.046 ms
RTT: 100 pings A → B without CLL	min: 0.178 ms ∅: 0.198 ms	max: 0.231 ms σ: 0.012 ms

tication of packets with CLL apparently has virtually no effect on the achievable data rate in 100 Mbit LANs, which proves the feasibility of our approach.

By comparing the CPU utilization with and without CLL being used, we assess the induced additional CPU load. The overhead of piping the packets through the user-mode and computing the HMAC turns out to be entirely admissible. Even when enabling the block cipher, host A still has a quarter of its CPU time left for other tasks when processing packets at full wire-speed. The faster host B (one CPU core active) runs with a CPU utilization of only one third in the same situation. Just like the TCP throughput, the RTT measured when running CLL in the Twofish / HMAC(MD5) configuration is very satisfactory. On average it is 0.38 ms, i.e., only twice the ordinary RTT without CLL. It should thus not represent a drawback for any typical application scenario.

2.6.3 Gigabit Ethernet and Parallelization

During the last few years we see the trend towards Gigabit Ethernet since almost all off-the-shelf computers are already equipped with Gigabit NICs. From the results above, it is evident that with only a single CPU core CLL cannot achieve wire-speed throughput in a Gigabit LAN providing both authentication and encryption. In a bachelor thesis [Ger12], we have thus investigated how the cryptographic processing of unicast transmissions can be parallelized in CLL on modern multi-core processors. Following the *boss/worker model* [NBF96], we have extended the original implementation by a *thread pool*. Using a packet queue, the boss thread delegates all incoming and outgoing unicast IP packets to multiple worker threads that perform the actual cryptographic processing of the packet, i.e., encryption / decryption and HMAC computation. Usually, there should be at least as many worker threads as there are CPU cores available. The packet queue ensures that all packets belonging to the same SA are delivered in the correct order. Due to a number of inherent dependencies, special attention had to be paid to synchronization issues.

With the original CLL implementation we measured in the RC6 / HMAC(MD5) configuration in a Gigabit LAN a throughput of 278 Mbit/s on an Intel Xeon X3360 2.83 GHz quad-core CPU running Windows 7 64-bit, while the parallelized version achieved a throughput of 557 Mbit/s using 4 and 580 Mbit/s using 8 worker threads respectively.

We observed that the additional synchronization overhead induced by parallelization has a great impact on performance since by far not all CPU time was consumed by the cryptographic and packet handling routines. We thus believe that a more elaborate implementation of the underlying thread pool can achieve even a higher throughput and will draw much closer to the (theoretical) 1000 Mbit/s mark.

2.7 Chapter Summary

In this chapter, we have introduced the Cryptographic Link Layer (CLL). CLL employs public-key cryptography to identify all hosts in the Ethernet LAN based on their IP/MAC address pairs. It safeguards the packets transmitted between them against different spoofing attacks and eavesdropping. Pairs of hosts willing to communicate first establish security associations by an extension of the ARP handshake. In the course of this, the hosts authenticate each other, exchange cryptographic parameters, and negotiate symmetric session keys to protect their following unicast packets with a message authentication code and an optional block cipher. Broadcast packets are also secured by CLL using digital signatures. When IP addresses are to be configured dynamically, CLL extends DHCP to automatically issue host certificates with the leased IP address. At the same time, CLL also adds authentication to DHCP and safeguards it against various attacks.

We have implemented CLL on both Windows and Linux without modifying the existing protocol stack. Backward compatibility to ordinary, unsecured hosts can be enabled to support a step-by-step migration and retain legacy devices. The evaluation of CLL demonstrated the excellent performance of our protocol in a 100 Mbit Ethernet LAN, where it achieved wire-speed throughput and short round-trip times. Moreover, we have recently extended our CLL implementation by a thread pool to parallelize the cryptographic processing of unicast packets on modern multi-core processors. This extension enables CLL to keep up with the achievable throughput rate even in Gigabit Ethernet.

Chapter 3

Counter-Flooding: DoS Protection for Public-Key Handshakes in LANs

In the previous chapter, we have introduced a comprehensive security protocol for LANs that protects against eavesdropping, spoofing, and DoS attacks on ARP and DHCP. CLL employs public-key cryptography during the setup phase—in particular digital signatures along with certificates—to perform authentication and exchange keying material. Examples of other LAN security protocols that also rely on public-key cryptography are IEEE 802.1X (EAPOL) [IEE04b] for port-based network access control being used especially in wireless networks by IEEE 802.11i (WPA2) [IEF04a] and *SEcure Neighbor Discovery (SEND)* [AKZN05] for IPv6. However, since public-key operations are very expensive in comparison to symmetric-key primitives like block ciphers and hash functions, they may constitute a new target for DoS attacks. Especially on the link layer an attacker can freely take on different identities (i.e., sender addresses) and send the victim host a flood of bogus connection requests, each one requiring to perform an expensive public-key operation. He may also impersonate another machine that answers a request and flood thousands of fake replies containing wrong signatures or certificates. The victim host would then become overloaded and very likely could not process the requests originating from benign hosts any more. Existing DoS protection schemes turn out to have drawbacks in environments with an eavesdropping attacker where initially no address authenticity exists. Is vulnerability to DoS attacks really the price to pay for employing public-key cryptography in LANs?

Chapter 3 Counter-Flooding: DoS Protection for Public-Key Handshakes in LANs

In this chapter, we propose a countermeasure against DoS flooding attacks on public-key handshakes in wired and wireless LANs. The idea is to configure on each host a reasonable threshold of signatures (or certificates) to be checked per second without overloading its CPU. A benign host trying to initiate an authentication handshake to a victim system being currently under a flooding attack reacts to this aggression by flooding itself multiple copies of its request packet for a short period. We call this approach *counter-flooding*. The attacked host collects all incoming request packets for a certain time interval and afterwards processes only those packets having the largest number of duplicates.

Usually the benign host has to flood its request packet only for some tens of milliseconds to ensure that it will be definitely processed by the victim. The key point is that the adversary cannot deliver many duplicates without, at the same time, reducing the victim's workload, i.e., the number of distinct signatures to verify. Interestingly, the bandwidth of the underlying link, i.e., the maximum rate at which the victim may receive request packets, does not influence the parameters of our counter-flooding approach. We take advantage of broadcast transmissions to detect DoS flooding attacks and run our counter-flooding defense only when necessary. We show that our duplicate-based selection policy for incoming requests outperforms a probabilistic arbitration mechanism. The practical applicability of our approach is underlined through flooding experiments with different Ethernet switches. In addition we demonstrate how IEEE 802.3x flow control can protect from DoS flooding attacks attempting to significantly degrade TCP throughput due to excessive packet loss. The main results of this chapter have been published in [JSM09].

The rest of the chapter is structured as follows. In the next section, we discuss existing approaches to protecting hosts against resource depletion through a flood of bogus request packets. Section 3.2 presents the design of the counter-flooding mechanism. In Section 3.3, we describe a queuing extension for our scheme and assess impact and quality of counter-flooding. Section 3.4 provides experimental results for bandwidth division during a flooding attack in switched Ethernet. In Section 3.5, we finally conclude this chapter with a short summary.

3.1 Related Work

Comprehensive surveys on DoS / DDoS attacks and proposed defense mechanisms can be found in [PLR07, DM04, MR04]. The authors of [PLR07] classify four categories of defense: (1) attack prevention, (2) attack detection, (3) attack source identification, and (4) attack reaction. Our counter-flooding mechanism falls into the last category. It is a currency-based approach. The host under attack demands from its clients to pay in some currency—in our case bandwidth—before spending itself resources to process their incoming requests. In the following we take a closer look on existing currency-based DoS defense mechanisms and point out their shortcomings if applied in LAN environments.

In [JB99], Juels and Brainard introduced *client puzzles* to protect servers from TCP SYN flooding attacks. Being under attack, a server distributes to its clients cryptographic puzzles in a stateless manner asking them to reverse a one-way hash function by brute force. The difficulty of the puzzle is chosen depending on the attack strength. Only after receiving a correct solution from the client the server allocates resources for the dangling TCP connection. The idea of CPU-bound client puzzles has been applied to authentication protocols in general by Aura et al. in [ANL01]. An implementation of client puzzles to protect the TLS handshake against DoS is described in [DS01]. However, the application of client puzzles itself may become the new target for an attacker if no address authenticity is provided by the underlying layers. The adversary can mount a second flooding attack against the clients of the defending host by overwhelming them with bogus puzzles pretending to come from the defending host. Depending on the chosen puzzle difficulty, even a modest puzzle packet rate may be sufficient to prevent the clients from solving the authentic puzzle set by the defending host. The ability to eavesdrop on the LAN traffic alleviates the puzzle attack since the attacker gets to know the clients performing currently an authentication handshake.

A systematic survey on DoS attacks in wireless IEEE 802.11 networks exploiting MAC and physical layer vulnerabilities is provided in [BT09]. The authors also discuss and compare available countermeasures. Martinovic et al. [MZS06, MZW$^+$08] addressed DoS attacks aiming to exhaust the access point's (AP) resources by flooding it with fake authentication requests. In [MZS06] they proposed a scheme called *Early MAC Address Binding* to protect the IEEE 802.11i / 802.1X handshakes. It involves a Diffie-Hellman

Chapter 3 Counter-Flooding: DoS Protection for Public-Key Handshakes in LANs

key exchange yielding a temporary message authentication code for the otherwise unsecured handshake frames and a cookie mechanism to bind the authentication requests to MAC addresses. However, this countermeasure only raises the bar for a successful DoS attack, but does not provide a complete protection. In [MZW+08] the authors suggested *wireless client puzzles* to be distributed by a defending AP to joining stations. To support highly heterogeneous stations these puzzles are not CPU-bound like in Juels' scheme. Instead of inverting a one-way function, a station has to measure the signal strength of the links to its neighbors and to find out those neighbors, whose link reaches a certain *Neighborhood Signal Threshold (NST)*. The NST is randomly chosen and frequently changed by the AP. A station replying with a wrong solution is detected by its neighbors, which thereupon issue a warning to the AP. However, similarly to the client puzzle attack described above, an adversary may impersonate the AP and announce many different NST values thus sabotaging the verification. The assumption that already authenticated stations are always benign and do not purposely issue false warnings may also not hold for some scenarios. In contrast, our counter-flooding mechanism does not require any trust. It would provide a viable protection for IEEE 802.11i / 802.1X handshakes.

Using bandwidth as a currency to defend against application-level distributed DoS attacks was proposed by Walfish et al. in [WVB+06]. The idea of their defense mechanism called *speak-up* is the following: a victimized server asks its clients to open a separate payment channel and to send through it some dummy bytes to the server. Each time the server is ready to process a new client request, it holds a virtual auction and selects the client that has sent the most bytes so far. At the same time the corresponding payment channel is terminated. While speak-up operates at the application layer and requires the establishment of TCP connections, our counter-flooding approach is more low level and deals with single packets. Speak-up implicitly relies on address authenticity to assign the payment, i.e., the received dummy bytes, to the corresponding client request. In the considered LAN scenario an (eavesdropping) attacker can break the speak-up mechanism by impersonating the benign clients and sending fake requests to the defending server which will likely spend the clients' payment to process the fake request instead of the genuine one. Unlike speak-up, our counter-flooding approach is resistant against this impersonation attack since a client pays by sending multiple copies of its request.

Here the payment cannot be spent without processing the genuine request itself.

In [GKTV04], Gunter et al. introduced a broadcast authentication protocol with DoS protection and packet loss tolerance based on digital signatures. To defend against a flood of fake signature packets the receiver checks each incoming signature only with a certain probability while the benign host sends multiple copies of his signature packet to raise its chances on verification. However, the authors calculate the required number of duplicate packets for a benign sender to succeed with high probability by making the unrealistic assumption that all copies will arrive at the receiver contiguously in a single pile without being intermixed with the attacker's signature packets. In contrast, we do not assume any special packet order in our counter-flooding approach and provide bounds on the number of duplicates to deterministically guarantee the processing of the good packet at the receiver. Our duplicate-based arbitration scheme turns out to be more efficient than random checking.

3.2 Design of Counter-Flooding

3.2.1 Goal: Safeguarding the Public-Key Handshake

Table 3.1: Symmetric vs. asymmetric key cryptography.

operation	speed
HMAC (MD5)	362.4 MB/s [371 100 pkt/s]
HMAC (SHA-1)	290.2 MB/s [297 170 pkt/s]
AES	135.8 MB/s [139 060 pkt/s]
RSA-1024 verify	10 676 pkt/s
RSA-2048 verify	3663 pkt/s
RSA-3072 verify	1972 pkt/s
RSA-4096 verify	1135 pkt/s
DSA-1024 verify	946 pkt/s
DSA-2048 verify	312 pkt/s

Table 3.1 compares the speed of symmetric versus asymmetric cryptography to authenticate 1 KB packets at the receiver. For the benchmark we used the popular crypto

Chapter 3 Counter-Flooding: DoS Protection for Public-Key Handshakes in LANs

library OpenSSL [Ope] on an Intel Core 2 Duo 2.66 GHz machine running 32-bit Linux (one CPU core active). The public exponent employed for RSA signatures was 65 537. Using an HMAC, current computers can easily authenticate incoming packets at full link-speed in IEEE 802.11g wireless networks, in 100 Mbit and even in 1 Gbit Ethernet LANs. Symmetric encryption/decryption using a block cipher like AES is also quite fast. In contrast, depending on the chosen modulus size, the verification of RSA signatures may already become a bottleneck at link speeds far below the 100 Mbit mark. Checking DSA signatures is even slower. Note that in public-key cryptography, the workload is primary determined by the number of packets and not by their size.

The benchmark results indicate that network communication protected by symmetric key cryptography (like message authentication code and block cipher) is in general not vulnerable to DoS flooding attacks, since the employed algorithms are usually fast enough to process packets at full link-speed. On the other hand the verification of digital signatures (or certificates) is quite slow. Thus we suppose that public-key authentication handshakes, which are often performed in the setup phase before switching to symmetric key cryptography, may be sabotaged by flooding the victim host with connection request packets containing bogus signatures. Our goal is therefore to protect the computationally expensive public-key handshake against DoS. In more general terms, we want to ensure the successful processing of important, infrequently sent genuine signature packets (be it handshake or status messages) despite of attackers flooding fake packets.

3.2.2 Basic Idea

We define for all hosts in the LAN a common threshold f for the maximum number of signature packets received per second during normal operation. f usually depends on the employed security protocol and the network size. If this threshold is exceeded, the receiver is considered to be under a DoS flooding attack and the counter-flooding protection mechanism gets invoked. Conversely, when the rate of incoming signature packets falls below the threshold f again, we return back to normal mode. In broadcast networks the benign sender A of a signature packet addressed to an attacked host B can overhear all the packets delivered to B and detect whether the threshold has been exceeded. In other networks, e. g., in switched Ethernet, one can instead prescribe that valid signature packets must always be sent to the broadcast MAC address to achieve the same effect. In this case A's MAC address must be stated in the packet's payload and A will drop any signature packet addressed directly to its own MAC address. A different approach for A would be to consider B as being attacked, if B does not reply to or acknowledge A's signature packet even after several retransmissions. However, in that case host A cannot exclude that there is no attack and B is simply currently offline.

When being under attack, host B divides the time into periods of length t (in the order of milliseconds) and collects all incoming signature packets in each period. Duplicate packets are stored only once. The queue maintains a duplicate counter for each packet stating how many times it has been received during the current period. Depending on B's CPU power (and its average load) the user configures a *verification threshold* of v signature checks per period t. This determines the maximum amount of CPU power B is willing to spend on the verification of signature packets. At the end of the current period all queued packets except for the v packets with the highest duplicate counter value are dropped. The remaining v packets have "won" the selection and their signatures will be verified during the next period. This verification can either be performed quickly at high CPU load straight at the beginning of the next period or it can be spread over the whole period length t.

We use bandwidth as a currency and request host A to flood its genuine signature packet addressed to victim B for a short time $p \leq t$ to ensure that it will definitely be processed. Figure 3.1 illustrates this approach. The intuition behind counter-flooding is to combat the attacker using his own weapons by verifying only those packets, that have a large number of duplicates. In LANs we can usually assume that host A and the attacker have equal or at least similar bandwidth capabilities. Therefore, the saboteur cannot afford to deliver a large number of different fake signature packets while simultaneously maintaining for all these packets a duplicate counter value as high as the value of A's packet in victim B's queue. The higher the bandwidth of host A's counter-flooding measure, the shorter we can choose the period length t and the required flooding duration p, i. e., the faster A's signature packet will be processed. Like the attacker, host A will usually flood at full link speed.

Chapter 3 Counter-Flooding: DoS Protection for Public-Key Handshakes in LANs

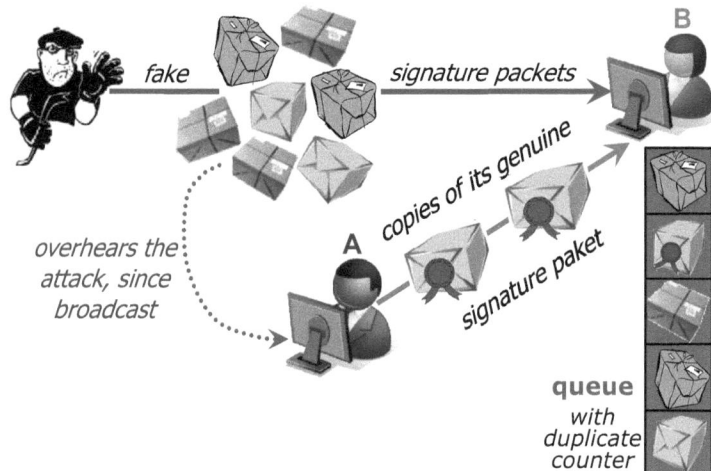

Figure 3.1: The counter-flooding approach.

3.2.3 Bandwidth vs. Packet Count

Host B's verification threshold v is expressed in the number of signature packets, while bandwidth is a measure for the number of bytes transferred per time unit. The attacker may try to gain an advantage over host A by flooding small signature packets without payload and—having the same link speed as A—hereby deliver more signature packets to victim B. For example, the length of an RSA-1024 signature is 128 bytes while the Maximum Transmission Unit (MTU) in Ethernet LANs usually is 1500 bytes (in Gigabit Ethernet even up to 9000 bytes). We address this issue by prescribing that valid signature packets must be padded with zeros to have full MTU size. This way all signature packets have equal size and we reduce the rate at which the attacker can deliver fake packets right from the start.

3.2.4 Determining the Flooding Duration

Now we determine the required flooding duration p for host A to guarantee that victim B will process its signature packet. Let b be the bandwidth of the links in the given network

3.2 Design of Counter-Flooding

expressed in the number of full MTU packets that can be transmitted per second. In case of a switched Ethernet both A and the attacker can send packets addressed to B at full rate b simultaneously, but the switch will deliver only half of the packets. The rest will be dropped due to queue overflow. A fair arbitration mechanism which serves all input ports in equal shares in case of an overload condition at an output port is the design goal of every good switch [Sei00]. Under ideal conditions victim B should therefore receive approximately the same number of packets from A and the attacker. We experimentally examine this aspect in Section 3.4. When operating in a wireless environment all senders have to share the available bandwidth b. Assuming a (somewhat) fair medium access control [BWK00] both A and the attacker should achieve approximately the same throughput and packet delivery rate with $\frac{b}{2}$ as the optimum if no other senders are active. However, our counter-flooding mechanism does not require a fair bandwidth division between host A and the attacker. Host A may send and deliver its signature packets at a lower rate than the attacker because of other packet flows dispatched by A or because of an unfair switch or medium access control. The only assumption we make is that host A can always achieve a packet delivery rate of at least $k \cdot b$ where $0 < k < 1$. That is, factor k denotes A's minimum link share with respect to signature packets addressed to B during the counter-flooding action.

Having the downlink bandwidth b victim B may receive up to $b \cdot t$ signature packets during a period of length t where at least $k \cdot b \cdot p$ duplicate packets originate from host A. From all received signature packets only v packets having the highest duplicate counters will be selected for verification. In total there can be no more than $\frac{bt}{kbp}$ packets having a duplicate counter equal or greater to the number of duplicates of A's packet. Thus if the inequality

$$\frac{bt}{kbp} \leq v \tag{3.1}$$

holds, host A's signature packet will be definitely among the v packets selected for verification during the next period. For the flooding duration $p \leq t$ we now get

$$p \geq \frac{t}{kv} \quad \Leftrightarrow \quad \frac{p}{t} \geq \frac{1}{kv} \tag{3.2}$$

where the condition $kv \geq 1$ must be fulfilled.

So far we have implicitly assumed that the hosts A and B are time synchronized and

Chapter 3 Counter-Flooding: DoS Protection for Public-Key Handshakes in LANs

A exactly knows when for B a new period begins. But a time synchronization between the hosts in the range of milliseconds is usually unrealistic. We address this issue by extending the flooding duration p to $p' = 2p$ and eliminate the dependency on time synchronization. This way host A definitely hits the beginning of a new period t and contributes to it with its duplicates for a time span of at least p.

3.2.5 Choosing the Parameters

The first step is to estimate the factor k. In case of a single attacker, one host performing counter-flooding, and a fair bandwidth division between the two k is 0.5. However, there can be multiple attackers (say, up to g) and/or several hosts (say, up to h) performing counter-flooding simultaneously for the same victim host. In this general case, assuming a fair bandwidth division, k can be set to $\frac{1}{g+h}$. To address possible unfairness in the bandwidth division we now introduce an *unbalance factor* u, $0 < u \leq 1$, and propose for k the expression $\frac{u}{g+h}$. The unbalance can be attributed to a suboptimal switch behavior or medium access control but also to the uplink of host A being concurrently used by some other packet flows. A reasonable value for u may be, for example, 0.5 or 0.3. The value for g depends on the network size and the (empiric) threat level, while h is primary determined by the number of hosts sending a signature packet to the same destination and the frequency of these packets.

So far we have not considered the impact of other packet flows occupying bandwidth on the victim's downlink. In a switched Ethernet these are all the other packets addressed to victim B, while in a wireless environment the remaining packet transmissions of the whole network altogether reduce the victim's downlink bandwidth available for signature packets. However, since the flooding duration p does not depend on the link bandwidth b, we can still use our model if we assume that b is not the physical bandwidth of the network links, but the bandwidth of the victim's downlink currently occupied by the flooded signature packets.

Now that we know k, we select a global value for v such that the inequality $kv \geq 1$ is fulfilled. We propose to set $v_{glob} = \frac{4}{k}$ yielding $\frac{p}{t} \geq \frac{1}{4}$ to have some latitude when choosing p. The last step is to select t large enough so that the majority of hosts in the network can verify v_{glob} signature packets in t without getting overloaded. Each user can now configure on its machine a local value for v, which may be of course larger (fast CPU) but also smaller (slow CPU) than the global value. In the first case the victim host will be robust against an overestimate of k, i.e., against a more powerful attack. In the second case it may fail to process host A's signature packet. But we can deal with hosts having a low v_{loc} value by increasing the flooding duration p up to the period length t. If victim B does not reply to or acknowledge A's signature packet, host A can perform counter-flooding repeatedly doubling each time the value for p in case of failure. Having $v_{glob} = \frac{4}{k}$ and $v_{loc} \geq \frac{1}{4} v_{glob}$ host A needs to double p at most twice (yielding $p = t$) to guarantee that victim B will definitely process its signature packet. Without time synchronization the real flooding duration remains, of course, $p' = 2p$.

To give an impression for the practical feasibility of the counter-flooding mechanism in an office LAN consisting of, e.g., 100 off-the-shelf computers we now calculate the real flooding duration p' using the following values: up to $g = 3$ attackers, up to $h = 2$ hosts performing counter-flooding simultaneously for the same victim, unbalance factor $u = 0.4$, $k = \frac{u}{g+h} = 0.08$, $v = \frac{4}{k} = 50$, verifying RSA-2048 signatures on a 2.66 GHz CPU (see Table 3.1) with an average CPU load of $25\% \Rightarrow t = \frac{50}{0.25 \cdot 3663} = 54.6$ ms. This yields $p \geq \frac{t}{kv} = 13.7$ ms and $p' = 2p \geq 27.4$ ms. Counter-flooding ensures that in case of a DoS attack victim B will process host A's signature packet with a delay of less than $p + 2t = 122.9$ ms (hitting the beginning of a new time period t, collecting packets during a full period, and verifying v signatures during the next period).

3.3 More Details

3.3.1 Reducing the Queue Size

During the period t the victim host needs to queue all incoming *different* signature packets. Depending on the link bandwidth b the memory requirement might be an issue for low-end and embedded systems. However, since all valid signature packets are padded to have maximum MTU size, only the meaningful part of the packet has to be stored. Furthermore we propose to significantly reduce the required memory footprint by employing a cryptographic hash function. The idea is to keep only v full packets—those having currently the largest duplicate counter—in the queue, while all other packets are represented by their hash value. A digest size of 64 or 80 bits should be large enough to avoid collisions. Then only 8 or 10 bytes (instead of, e.g., 1000 bytes) are required per packet. When more duplicates of a packet, which is right now represented in the queue only by its digest, arrive, it gets enqueued as a full packet and takes up the place of one of the v packets having a lower duplicate counter. The ousted packet is replaced by its digest. The described algorithm ensures that the v packets with the largest duplicate counters are definitely available for verification at the end of period t.

3.3.2 Impact of Counter-Flooding on Network Performance

We believe that the impact of counter-flooding on the overall network performance is negligible. Our DoS countermeasure is very goal-oriented. It comes into action only in case of a real flooding attack, only when performing an authentication handshake, and only for a very short period of time in the order of 20–60 ms. Ordinary file transfer usually occupies a large portion of bandwidth for much longer periods. Another point is that by flooding *broadcast* packets at full speed (or generally in wireless networks) a single attacker can already induce an overload situation for the whole network. In this case counter-flooding cannot increase the network load any more since it has already reached the maximum. Here the bandwidth occupied by counter-flooding comes at the cost of the attacker's bandwidth.

3.3.3 Comparison to a Probabilistic Arbitration Scheme

Counter-flooding employs a deterministic arbitration scheme at victim B, which selects the signature packets with the highest number of duplicates for verification. We now compare this scheme to a probabilistic one inspired by [GKTV04], in which from the n packets (including duplicates) received during period t the victim host *randomly* chooses v packets for verification. Let in this case m be the number of packets originating from host A. Then, using simple combinatorics, the probability that at least one of

3.4 Flooding Experiments in Switched Ethernet

A's packets will be among the v selected ones can be expressed by

$$\beta = \frac{\sum_{i=0}^{v-1} \binom{m}{v-i}\binom{n-m}{i}}{\binom{n}{v}}. \qquad (3.3)$$

Taking the parameters $k = 0.08$, $v = 50$, $t = 54.6$ ms and $p = 13.7$ ms from the example in Section 3.2.5, we compute now the probability β in a 100 Mbit and 1 Gbit Ethernet LAN. Assuming a frame size of 1518 bytes at the link layer, we get $n = 450$, $m = 9$ for $b = 100$ Mbit/s and use $n = 4500$, $m = 90$ for $b = 1$ Gbit/s. This yields a probability β of only 65.7% (100 Mbit) and 63.8% (1 Gbit) respectively. When maximizing m by setting $p - t$ (i.e., quadrupling the flooding duration) the verification probability β reaches a value of 98.8% and 98.5% respectively.

This comparison demonstrates that our deterministic duplicate-counter-based selection policy clearly outperforms the probabilistic one which does not distinguish between different and duplicate packets. In the probabilistic approach the chances for verification decrease when the bandwidth increases, while the deterministic strategy does not depend on the link speed. The advantage of the duplicate-counter-based strategy can be explained as follows: the verification of one forged signature packet eliminates the need to check a multiplicity of other forged packets, namely all its duplicates, while each verification of a randomly selected packet excludes only this single packet from the candidate queue.

3.4 Flooding Experiments in Switched Ethernet

In this section we present the results from flooding experiments with Ethernet switches to examine the bandwidth division between concurrent packet flows.

3.4.1 IEEE 802.3x Flow Control

To address the problem of switch congestion resulting in packet loss, the IEEE 802.3x Task Force specified for full duplex Ethernet a hop-by-hop flow control scheme—the

PAUSE function [IEE05, Sei00]. Whenever the switch receives packets faster than they can be forwarded to the output port(s), it emits a special PAUSE frame at the corresponding input port(s). The PAUSE frame asks the station at the other end of the link to stop transmitting further packets for a specified amount of time. This enables the switch to empty its input buffer without discarding packets. Both the switch and the station's NIC must support flow control to take advantage of it. This is the case for the majority of today's hardware. However, flow control often needs to be activated manually in the NIC driver configuration.

Dealing with flooding attacks which usually provoke an overload condition at the switch, it seems important to take flow control into account for our experiments.

3.4.2 Bandwidth Division between Host A and Attacker

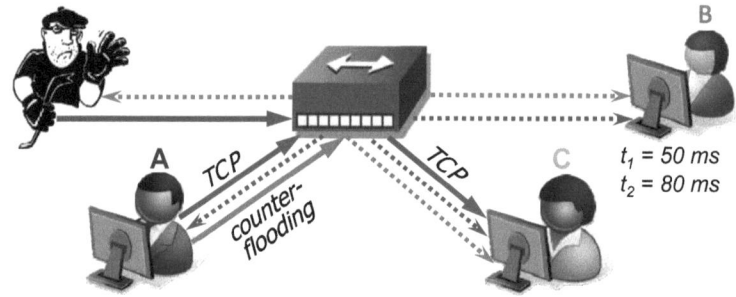

Figure 3.2: Bandwidth division experiments: counter-flooding broadcast packets with parallel TCP connection (CF_B TCP).

We examine the fairness of bandwidth division between the benign host A and the attacker when performing counter-flooding. This helps to properly choose the factor k. Using in turn three different switches we set up a LAN consisting of four hosts: the attacker, victim B, host A and another host C as shown in Figure 3.2. The hosts A, B, and C are notebooks equipped with an Intel Core 2 Duo 1.60 GHz CPU and an Intel 8256MM Gigabit NIC, while the attacker's machine has an Intel Core 2 Duo 2.66 GHz CPU with a Realtek 8111B Gigabit NIC. The first two switches, a LevelOne FSW-2205TX and a 3com OfficeConnect 8 Plus, operate at 100 Mbit. The third one, a

3Com OfficeConnect 5, provides Gigabit speed. Injecting and capturing raw Ethernet frames is performed by means of the *pcap* library [pca]. The attacker continuously floods maximum MTU packets at full link-speed addressed to victim B, which registers all packets received during time periods of length $t = 50$ ms in the first and $t = 80$ ms in the second measurement. Host A reacts to this aggression by counter-flooding maximum MTU packets for $p' = 2t$ to definitely hit a full period t at B. We record the number of packets received from A and the attacker during the second period of length t with packet contribution from both hosts. This is the desired full period with A's packets. The number of A's packets divided by the total number of packets yields its bandwidth share k'. We measure k' under various conditions: counter-flooding unicast (CF_U) or broadcast (CF_B) packets, with flow control disabled (noFC) or enabled (FC), and having the entire uplink bandwidth available or running in parallel to a TCP connection which tries to send data to host C at maximum speed. The attacker always operates with flow control disabled. However, he adheres to the policy whether valid signature packets are broadcasted or unicasted. Otherwise his fake packets can be detected based on the destination MAC address. For each configuration we perform 15 runs and state the ranges of the measured values for k' in Table 3.2. In Gigabit Ethernet switching off flow control has no effect in case of the two employed NIC chipsets—in remains in fact enabled. Therefore there are no test results without flow control for the Gigabit switch.

Evaluating the results, the general observation to be made is that host A's bandwidth share did never drop below 33% (entire uplink channel available) and 19% (concurrent TCP flow) respectively. Hence, the bandwidth division can be assessed as reasonably fair and, more important, an acceptably large lower bound for factor k exists. Using the expression $k = \frac{u}{g+h}$ proposed in Section 3.2.5 with $g = 1$ and $h = 1$, the unbalance factor u yielding $k = 0.19$ would amount to 0.38.

Without a concurrent TCP flow, when using the first or the third switch, the bandwidth division between host A and the attacker is almost optimal, that is $k' \approx 50\%$, in all runs. Flow control has no significant effect on fairness in case of the first switch. However, the second switch shows striking fluctuations in bandwidth division when flooding unicast packets without flow control and it drops almost all attacker's unicast packets when A has flow control enabled. That is, this switch favors stations which perform flow control.

Table 3.2: Bandwidth division during counter-flooding under different conditions.

conditions	host A's bandwidth share k'					
	LevelOne FSW-2205TX 100 Mbit		3com OfficeConnect 8 Plus 100 Mbit		3Com OfficeConnect 5 1 Gbit	
	$t = 50\ ms$	$t = 80\ ms$	$t = 50\ ms$	$t = 80\ ms$	$t = 50\ ms$	$t = 80\ ms$
CF_U noFC	47.8% – 51.3%	49.1% – 51.4%	33.5% – 60.7%	33.4% – 66.9%	—	—
CF_U FC	52.5% – 54.9%	52.4% – 52.5%	95.8% – 99.7%	97.5% – 100%	49.7% – 49.9%	49.6% – 49.7%
CF_B noFC	47.5% – 52.5%	47.7% – 52.5%	49.9% – 50.0%	50.0% – 50.1%	—	—
CF_B FC	55.0% – 55.2%	54.1% – 55.0%	46.7% – 50.1%	50.0% – 50.1%	49.9% – 50.1%	50.1% – 50.6%
CF_U TCP noFC	19.1% – 23.6%	19.2% – 24.3%	20.9% – 37.1%	27.7% – 37.2%	—	—
CF_U TCP FC	23.2% – 27.8%	21.9% – 27.9%	28.5% – 36.6%	27.8% – 36.9%	27.1% – 33.9%	26.3% – 33.4%
CF_B TCP noFC	38.6% – 50.1%	40.0% – 52.1%	49.6% – 50.3%	49.8% – 53.6%	—	—
CF_B TCP FC	26.1% – 31.5%	25.3% – 29.4%	28.3% – 40.2%	29.4% – 38.7%	28.4% – 38.5%	28.6% – 37.6%

3.4 Flooding Experiments in Switched Ethernet

All test series with a concurrent TCP flow exhibit medium-strength fluctuations of A's bandwidth share. This is probably due to varying TCP throughput occupying more or less uplink bandwidth and maybe also due to short-time monopolization of A's uplink either by the TCP or the counter-flooding flow. If TCP congestion control does not throttle the sending rate, a fair use of A's uplink by TCP and counter-flooding as well as a fair arbitration mechanism in the switch would result in k' to amount to 25%. It is noticeable that in the broadcast test series without flow control k' is between 40% and 50%. We explain this by the fact that persistent packet loss in the overloaded switch forces TCP's congestion control to dramatically cut down its throughput, so that counter-flooding can occupy nearly the whole uplink. The fatal effect of flooding attacks on TCP throughput is subject of the next subsection.

3.4.3 Preventing DoS Flooding Attacks on TCP

Using the existing setup, we let the attacker flood at full speed unicast or broadcast packets of maximum size to victim B thereby completely occupying its downlink. While the attack is in progress, host A runs the TCP benchmark tool *ttcp* [TTC] sending data to victim B as fast as possible (40 KB buffer, 500 *send()* calls). We examine the impact of Ethernet flow control on the achievable TCP throughput by making measurements with and without flow control enabled at the hosts A and B. The attacker has flow control always switched off. Another test series is performed under normal conditions without a flooding attack to determine the baseline TCP throughput. For each configuration we perform 15 runs and present the ranges of the measured speeds in Table 3.3.

Table 3.3: Effect of Ethernet flow control on TCP throughput under a DoS flooding attack.

conditions	TCP throughput in MB/s		
	switch 1	switch 2	switch 3
noFC noDoS	11.32 – 11.33	11.32 – 11.33	—
FC noDoS	11.32 – 11.33	11.32 – 11.33	102.7 – 110.1
noFC DoS_U	0.294 – 0.607	0.117 – 0.138	—
FC DoS_U	5.91 – 5.94	10.47 – 10.63	52.94 – 53.16
FC DoS_B	5.93 – 5.96	10.54 – 10.56	44.29 – 44.62

Chapter 3 Counter-Flooding: DoS Protection for Public-Key Handshakes in LANs

Under normal conditions the TCP throughput achieves (almost) link-speed irrespective of whether IEEE 802.3x flow control is enabled or not. Without flow control the flooding attack succeeds in degrading TCP throughput by 95–99% due to packet loss which continuously triggers TCP's slow start mode. This constitutes a very severe DoS attack since the majority of applications employ TCP. However, Ethernet flow control is capable to maintain a TCP throughput of more than 50% of the regular speed, as it avoids packet loss.

3.5 Chapter Summary

In this chapter, we have proposed a countermeasure against DoS flooding attacks on public-key handshakes in LANs. If an adversary tries to overwhelm a victim host by a flood of invalid signature packets requiring expensive verification, a benign host ensures the processing of its genuine signature packet by flooding itself copies of this packet for a short period. We have provided bounds for counter-flooding to succeed and shown experimentally that in switched Ethernet a reasonable fair bandwidth division between concurrent flows is usually ensured. Moreover, we have shown how IEEE 802.3x flow control can protect from flooding attacks attempting to significantly degrade TCP throughput. We believe that this finding and especially our link layer security protocol CLL extended by the counter-flooding protection for its public-key handshake will pave the way for secure and DoS-resistant communication in LANs.

Chapter 4

Non-Parallelizable and Non-Interactive Client Puzzles

Protocols and services that perform authentication and key exchange relying on expensive public-key cryptography or involve complex database queries are likely vulnerable to DoS attacks. By flooding valid-looking requests, for example SSL / TLS, IPsec, or CLL authentication handshakes, an attacker seeks to overload his victim. But even services that do not involve expensive operations may be susceptible to DoS attacks that exploit worst-case behavior of classical data structures like hash tables [CW03]. In the previous chapter, we have introduced counter-flooding to protect public-key handshakes in LANs against DoS. We have pointed out that *client puzzles* [JB99, Bac02, ANL01]—the well-known countermeasure against resource exhaustion attacks in the Internet—have drawbacks if being applied in LANs where initially no address authenticity exists. In this chapter, we revisit the client puzzle approach and propose a novel puzzle construction that offers some advantages over existing schemes. Its application is not limited to LANs. The content of this chapter has been published in [JM11] and an extended version of that paper is currently under review [JM12a].

We briefly recall the concept of client puzzles: A server being under attack processes requests only from those clients that themselves spend resources in solving a cryptographic puzzle and submit the right solution. Puzzle verification must be cheap, while the puzzle difficulty can be tuned from easy to hard. By imposing a computational task on the client the victimized server dramatically cuts down the number of valid requests that the attacker can emit. However, benign hosts having only a single request

Chapter 4 Non-Parallelizable and Non-Interactive Client Puzzles

are hardly penalized. A widely-used cost function for client puzzles is the reversal of a one-way hash function by brute force. Verifying such a puzzle involves only a single hash operation.

Client puzzles can be *interactive* or *non-interactive*. In the first case the server constructs the puzzle upon receiving a request and demands from the client to solve it before continuing with the protocol. In the latter case the client constructs the puzzle by itself, solves it and attaches the solution to its request. An important characteristic of client puzzles is *granularity*, i.e., the ability to finely adjust the puzzle difficulty to different levels. Another desirable property is *non-parallelizability*, which prevents an attacker from obtaining the solution faster than scheduled by distributing the puzzle to multiple CPU cores or to other compromised machines [TBFN07, SvB07, Kv10]. Existing client puzzle schemes are either parallelizable, coarse-grained, or can be used only interactively. Interactive puzzles have the drawback that the packet with the puzzle parameters sent from server to client lacks authentication. A second DoS attack against the clients with faked packets pretending to come from the defending server and containing bogus puzzle parameters may thwart the clients' connection attempts. Such a counterattack becomes feasible if no address authenticity is provided by the underlying layers, e.g., if operating at the link layer. To the best of our knowledge, no puzzle scheme proposed in the literature provides all the desired properties.

We introduce a novel scheme for client puzzles based on the computation of square roots modulo a prime. *Modular square root puzzles* are non-parallelizable, can be employed both interactively and non-interactively, and provide polynomial granularity. We construct the puzzle for a particular request by assigning to it a unique quadratic residue a modulo a prime. Then the client solves the puzzle by extracting the modular square root of a and sends it to the server as proof of work. Computation is performed by repeated squaring, which is assumed to be an intrinsically sequential process. Verifying the puzzle on the server side is easy—it requires a single modular squaring operation and a few hash operations. Puzzle difficulty can be tuned by selecting a larger or smaller prime modulus. We evaluate the performance of modular square root puzzles by benchmarking the verification throughput and the solution time for different levels of difficulty. The results demonstrate the feasibility of our approach to mitigate DoS attacks on hosts having a 1 or even 10 Gbit link. To compensate for raising verification costs in high-speed networks we strengthen our puzzle scheme by introducing a small bandwidth-based cost factor for the client. Furthermore, we also investigate the construction of client puzzles from modular cube roots.

The rest of this chapter is organized as follows. In the next section, we discuss existing approaches for DoS protection with the aid of puzzles. Section 4.2 introduces algorithms for computing modular square roots, investigates parallelization aspects, and forms the mathematical basis for our client puzzles. In Section 4.3, we then describe how to construct, solve and verify a modular square root puzzle, which can be employed in a non-interactive or interactive manner. Section 4.4 evaluates the performance of our puzzle scheme and extends it by a bandwidth-based cost factor. Finally, we conclude the chapter with a summary in Section 4.5.

4.1 Related Work

Hash-reversal puzzles [JB99, Bac02, ANL01] can be used both interactively and non-interactively. They are simple to construct and verify but have the disadvantage of being highly parallelizable and provide only exponential granularity. The task of reversing a one-way hash function by brute force can be easily distributed across many machines. To make them fine-grained Feng et al. propose *hint-based hash reversal puzzles* [FKFL05] where the server gives the client a hint about the range within which the solution lies. Thus, the granularity becomes linear. The drawback is that hint-based puzzles can be employed only interactively.

Waters et al. introduced a client puzzle scheme based on the Diffie-Hellman key exchange where puzzle construction and distribution are outsourced to a secure entity called *bastion* [WJHF04]. The bastion periodically issues puzzles for a specific number of virtual channels that are valid during the next time slot. Puzzle construction is quite expensive since it requires a modular exponentiation, but many servers can rely on puzzles distributed by the same bastion. A client solves a puzzle by computing the discrete logarithm through brute force testing—a task that is highly parallelizable. The granularity of the puzzle is linear. On the server side, verifying a puzzle involves a

Chapter 4 Non-Parallelizable and Non-Interactive Client Puzzles

table lookup and another costly modular exponentiation, which, however, is performed in advance during the previous time slot.

In [TBFN07], Tritilanunt et al. first reviewed existing client puzzle approaches and compared their properties. The authors then suggested a non-parallelizable client puzzle scheme based on the *subset sum problem*. The client solves the puzzle by applying Lenstra's lattice reduction algorithm LLL. However, the authors point out that the memory requirements for LLL are quite high, which results in some implementation issues. Puzzle verification is quite cheap. It takes one hash operation and about 25–100 additions. Subset sum puzzles are interactive and provide polynomial granularity. In contrast, our puzzle scheme can be also employed non-interactively, has a small memory footprint, and is easy to implement.

Non-parallelizable puzzles based on repeated squaring are well-known in timed-release cryptography. In [RSW96], Rivest et al. introduced interactive *time-lock puzzles* to encrypt messages that can be decrypted by others only after a pre-determined amount of time has passed. Like the RSA cryptosystem time-lock puzzles rely on the intractability of factoring large integers. Constructing a time-lock puzzle requires the server to perform an expensive modular exponentiation. Later in this thesis, in Chapter 6 in the context of our offline submission protocol, we will discuss Rivest's time-lock puzzles in more detail.

Seeking for a non-parallelizable (but still interactive) client puzzle scheme Karame and Čapkun adapted Rivest's puzzle scheme by employing an RSA key pair with small private exponent to reduce the costs for puzzle verification [Kv10]. The server must still perform a modular exponentiation but the number of multiplications is decreased by some factor, e.g., factor 12.8 for a 1024-bit modulus resulting in 120 modular multiplications instead of 1536. We find that these verification costs are nevertheless too high to provide a viable DoS protection for high-speed links. In contrast, verifying our modular square root puzzle takes only a single modular squaring operation.

With the discussed RSA based puzzle schemes we share the idea of a non-parallelizable solution function that relies on modular exponentiation. Apart from that, our approach is different and does not use any trapdoor information. In [DN92], Dwork and Naor mentioned the extraction of modular square roots as one of three candidate families of pricing functions to combat spam. Our main contribution here to counteract DoS attacks is the computation of modular square roots from so-called "hard" primes resulting in a novel scheme for non-parallelizable client puzzles.

In [CMSW09], Chen et al. gave a formal model for the security of client puzzles. Further client puzzle architectures are, e.g., [WR03, WR04, HGS+08, SvB07, TJ10]. Puzzle-based DoS defense mechanisms can also rely on other payment schemes than CPU cycles, for example on memory [ABMW05, DGN03, DMR06], bandwidth [WVB+06] (see Section 3.1), or human interaction where so-called *CAPTCHAs* [vABHL03] have become the most common technique. Besides DoS protection various other applications for computational puzzles have been proposed, e.g., mitigating spam [DN92, Bac02], uncheatable benchmarks [CLSY93], a zero-knowledge protocol for timed-release encryption and signatures [Mao01], or a timed commitment scheme for contract signing [BN00].

4.2 Modular Square Roots

4.2.1 Extracting Square Roots Modulo a Prime

Let p be an odd prime and $a \in \mathbb{Z}_p^*$ an integer, i.e., $1 \leq a \leq p-1$. The solution of the congruence $x^2 \equiv a \pmod{p}$ is called a *square root modulo p*. There exist either two solutions x and $-x$ or no solution. In the first case, a is named a *quadratic residue*, and in the latter case a *quadratic non-residue* modulo p. Half of the elements in $\mathbb{Z}_p^*$ are quadratic residues and the other half are quadratic non-residues. To express whether a is a quadratic residue or not the *Legendre symbol* $\left(\frac{a}{p}\right)$ is used. It is defined as being 1 if a is quadratic residue, -1 if a is a quadratic non-residue and 0 if operating in $\mathbb{Z}_p$ and $a = 0$. The Legendre symbol can be efficiently computed in $\mathcal{O}((\log p)^2)$ bit operations [Coh96, MvOV96].

Finding a square root modulo p is quite easy for half of the primes p, namely if $p \equiv 3 \pmod{4}$. In this case the solution is given by

$$x = a^{(p+1)/4} \bmod p. \tag{4.1}$$

Chapter 4 Non-Parallelizable and Non-Interactive Client Puzzles

For half of the remaining primes where $p \equiv 5 \ (mod \ 8)$ a less trivial, but also straightforward solution exists:

$$x = \begin{cases} a^{(p+3)/8} \ mod \ p & \text{if } a^{(p-1)/4} \ mod \ p = 1 \\ 2a(4a)^{(p-5)/8} \ mod \ p & \text{otherwise.} \end{cases} \quad (4.2)$$

The remaining case $p \equiv 1 \ (mod \ 8)$ is the most difficult one. However, there exist two well-known algorithms [BS96, NHSK09] to compute square roots modulo p for all primes p, namely the *Tonelli-Shanks method* [Ton91, Sha72] (see Algorithm 1 [MvOV96]) and the *Cipolla-Lehmer method* [Cip03, Leh69] (see Algorithm 2 [MvOV96]). The group-theoretic Tonelli-Shanks method has a running time of $\mathcal{O}((log \ p)^4)$ bit operations if $p-1$ contains a large power of two in its prime factorization. But for small s (see line 3) it runs in $\mathcal{O}((log \ p)^3)$ since in this case the for loop is executed only a small number of times. The Cipolla-Lehmer method is based on the theory of finite fields and works with polynomials over the field $\mathbb{Z}_p$. In contrast to the algorithm of Tonelli-Shanks its running time does not depend on the decomposition of $p-1$ and is always in $\mathcal{O}((log \ p)^3)$. Note that for primes p where s is very small the Tonelli-Shanks algorithm will outperform the Cipolla-Lehmer method, because an exponentiation in the polynomial ring $\mathbb{Z}_p[x]$ is more expensive than in $\mathbb{Z}_p$. Both algorithms have a probabilistic component, namely finding a quadratic non-residue modulo p. For the Tonelli-Shanks method this quadratic non-residue does not depend on a and can be precomputed if p is fixed. A random integer $b \in \mathbb{Z}_p$ is a quadratic non-residue with probability 0.5. In case of the Cipolla-Lehmer method we need to know a to find a suitable quadratic non-residue and the probability for succeeding with a random integer b is $0.5 - \frac{1}{2p}$ [BS96], which converges to 0.5 for large primes p. On average, two trials should suffice for both methods to find a quadratic non-residue. The time required for this test is negligible compared to the total computation of the square root. It is an open question whether randomization can be eliminated, although this will be possible if the extended Riemann hypothesis turns out to be true. So far modular square roots can be computed only in random polynomial time by a Las Vegas algorithm [BS96].

4.2 Modular Square Roots

Algorithm 1 Tonelli-Shanks: square roots modulo a prime p

Input: an odd prime p and an integer a, $1 \leq a \leq p-1$.
Output: the two square roots of a modulo p, provided a is a quadratic residue modulo p.

1: Compute the Legendre symbol $\left(\frac{a}{p}\right)$. **if** $\left(\frac{a}{p}\right) = -1$ **then print** "*a has no square roots modulo p*" and terminate.
2: Find a quadratic non-residue b modulo p at random, i.e., an integer b, $1 \leq b \leq p-1$, with $\left(\frac{b}{p}\right) = -1$.
3: Write $p - 1 = 2^s t$, where t is odd.
4: Compute $a^{-1} \ mod \ p$ by the extended Euclidean algorithm.
5: Set $c \leftarrow b^t \ mod \ p$ and $r \leftarrow a^{(t+1)/2} \ mod \ p$.
6: **for** $i = 1$ to $s - 1$ **do**
7:    Compute $d = (r^2 \cdot a^{-1})^{2^{s-i-1}} \ mod \ p$.
8:    **if** $d \equiv -1 \ (mod \ p)$ **then** set $r \leftarrow r \cdot c \ mod \ p$.
9:    Set $c \leftarrow c^2 \ mod \ p$.
10: **end for**
11: **return** $(r, -r)$

Algorithm 2 Cipolla-Lehmer: square roots modulo a prime p

Input: an odd prime p and an integer a, $1 \leq a \leq p-1$.
Output: the two square roots of a modulo p, provided a is a quadratic residue modulo p.

1: Compute the Legendre symbol $\left(\frac{a}{p}\right)$. **if** $\left(\frac{a}{p}\right) = -1$ **then print** "*a has no square roots modulo p*" and terminate.
2: Choose an integer $b \in \mathbb{Z}_p$ at random until $b^2 - 4a$ is a quadratic non-residue modulo p, i.e., $\left(\frac{b^2-4a}{p}\right) = -1$.
3: Let f be the polynomial $x^2 - bx + a$ in $\mathbb{Z}_p[x]$.
Compute $r = x^{(p+1)/2} \ mod \ f$. (Note: r will be an integer.)
4: **return** $(r, -r)$

Chapter 4 Non-Parallelizable and Non-Interactive Client Puzzles

4.2.2 Modular Exponentiation

Extracting a modular square root requires to perform modular exponentiations. This task can be accomplished by the basic *binary exponentiation method* (commonly referred to as square-and-multiply) or a more sophisticated algorithm like the *k-ary method* or the *sliding-window method* [MvOV96]. In case $p \equiv 3 \pmod 4$ only one modular exponentiation is needed. If $p \equiv 5 \pmod 8$ then two modular exponentiations have to be performed. Finally, if $p \equiv 1 \pmod 8$ the Tonelli-Shanks or Cipolla-Lehmer algorithm has to be applied. In the worst case, namely if s is large, the Tonelli-Shanks method carries out up to $\mathcal{O}(log\ p)$ modular exponentiations in the for loop and becomes quite inefficient. Primes $p \equiv 1 \pmod 8$ of appropriate size where the prime factorization of $p-1$ contains a large power of two can be easily found. We suggest Algorithm 3 for this purpose. In line 5 the function *IsProbablePrime()* repeatedly performs a randomized primality test, e.g., the Miller-Rabin test [Mil76, Rab80], to achieve a given error bound (which is less than 4^{-k} after k rounds in case of the Miller-Rabin test). Finding such a "hard" prime p with an error probability below 10^{-15} takes less than 50 msec for a 1031-bit prime (input: $l = 1024$) and less than 1 sec for a 2058-bit prime (input: $l = 2048$) on a modern 64-bit CPU.

Algorithm 3 Finding a "hard" prime for modular square roots
Input: minimal bit length l.
Output: the smallest prime p having at least l bits with $p - 1 = 2^s t$ where t is odd and s in $\mathcal{O}(log\ p)$.

1: set $i \leftarrow 1$
2: **repeat**
3:     $p = (2^{l-1} \cdot i) + 1$
4:     set $i \leftarrow i + 2$
5: **while not** *IsProbablePrime(p)*
6: **return** p

In the following, we thus concentrate on such "hard" primes and the Cipolla-Lehmer method, which ignores the structure of $p-1$. Here the computation consists of a single modular exponentiation $x^{(p+1)/2} \bmod f$, but with polynomials instead of integers. The modulus f is a polynomial of degree 2 with leading coefficient 1. How many modular multiplication / squaring operations on integers are involved in this exponentiation?

4.2 Modular Square Roots

First, we observe that if p is a "hard" prime the exponent $(p + 1)/2$ has the form $2^{s-1} \cdot i + 1$ where i is a small integer. Only some of the most significant bits and the least significant bit are set. Hence, the computation actually reduces to an exponentiation with a power-of-two exponent, where repeated squaring—a special case of the binary exponentiation—constitutes the most efficient technique. To compute $g^y \bmod n$ with $y = 2^k$ it takes k modular squarings and no additional multiplications while $\lfloor log\ y \rfloor$ is the lower bound for the number of multiplications to carry out a single exponentiation in a general group. Squaring a polynomial $ax + b$ of degree 1 over the field $\mathbb{Z}_p$ requires 3 modular integer multiplications / squarings. Reducing the resulting polynomial of degree 2 modulo f, i.e., performing a polynomial division, involves 2 modular multiplications and 2 modular subtractions on integers. While modular multiplication / squaring of N-bit numbers runs in $\mathcal{O}(N^2)$ (or in $\mathcal{O}(N^{1.585})$ with a sophisticated technique like Karatsuba's algorithm [KO62]), modular subtraction takes linear time, and thus is negligible. Altogether, the modular exponentiation in $\mathbb{Z}_p[x]$ takes about $5 \cdot log\ p$ modular multiplication / squaring operations on integers.

4.2.3 Non-Parallelizability

In all exponentiation algorithms the main workload accounts to repeatedly performing modular squarings. This is assumed to be an intrinsically sequential, i.e., non-parallelizable process since each next step requires the intermediate result from the previous one [RSW96]. Parallelization of the squaring operation itself cannot achieve a significant speedup either. Each squaring requires only trivial computational resources and any non-trivial scale of parallelization inside the squaring operation would be likely penalized by communication overhead among the processors [Mao01]. In complexity theory, the class P contains all decision problems that can be solved by a deterministic Turing machine in polynomial time. NC $\subseteq$ P represents the class of problems that can be efficiently solved by a parallel computer. However, it is still an open question whether modular exponentiation is P-complete, i.e., not in NC [AK88, Sor99]. Likewise, it is unknown if factoring is really not in P.

We now want to point out those parts of modular square root computation that are parallelizable. If applying the basic binary exponentiation method the $\frac{1}{2} \cdot log\ p$ multiply

Chapter 4 Non-Parallelizable and Non-Interactive Client Puzzles

steps can be performed in parallel to the $log\ p$ squaring steps. Thus, only $log\ p$ sequential modular squaring operations can be accounted for when extracting a square root modulo $p \equiv 3\ (mod\ 4)$. The same applies to the case $p \equiv 5\ (mod\ 8)$ where two modular exponentiations are performed (see Equation 4.2). Instead of evaluating $a^{(p-1)/4}\ mod\ p$ first and then deciding on which will be the second exponentiation, one could carry out all three modular exponentiations in parallel and then determine the correct square root instantly by checking the result of $a^{(p-1)/4}\ mod\ p$. When dealing with "hard" primes $p \equiv 1\ (mod\ 8)$ parallelization is also possible to some degree. We can do the 3 modular multiplications / squarings to square the polynomial simultaneously. Afterwards the 2 modular multiplications for polynomial division can be also performed in parallel. This results in about $2 \cdot log\ p$ sequential modular multiplications to compute a square root modulo a "hard" prime $p \equiv 1\ (mod\ 8)$ and takes more than twice as long as for other primes, since multiplying is somewhat slower than squaring [GMP]. Thus we have found a way to increase the time for square root extraction by more than factor 2, which cannot be diminished by raising the number of available processors.

4.3 Client Puzzles from Modular Square Roots

4.3.1 Constructing and Solving a Non-Interactive Puzzle

The benign host A having a request (e. g., an authentication handshake) to host B that is under a DoS attack constructs for its request a unique puzzle. We suppose that both parties share a list $L = \{p_1, ..., p_j\}$ of "hard" primes $p \equiv 1\ (mod\ 8)$ with different bit lengths which have been generated once and henceforth can be used by all hosts an unlimited number of times. The puzzle must be bound to A's request message m. Depending on the layer the protocol is operating at m may be an Ethernet frame, an IP datagram or a TCP/UDP segment. First, host A selects from the list L a prime p of appropriate bit length n and applies a cryptographic hash function H with digest length k on m recursively $c = \lceil \frac{n}{k} \rceil$ times to produce the $(n-1)$-bit digest

$$d = First_{n-1}(H(m)\ ||\ H(H(m))\ ||\ ...\ ||\ H^c(m)). \qquad (4.3)$$

4.3 Client Puzzles from Modular Square Roots

Here $||$ denotes the concatenation of two bit strings and $First_i$ extracts the first i bits from a bit string. Next host A considers d as a $(n-1)$-bit number and computes the Legendre symbol $\left(\frac{d}{p}\right)$ to check whether d is a quadratic residue modulo p. If it turns out to be a quadratic non-residue, d is decremented by one until the quadratic residue a is found:

Algorithm 4 Assigning a unique quadratic residue to the digest d, method 1
---
set $a \leftarrow d$
while $\left(\frac{a}{p}\right) = -1$ **do**
   set $a \leftarrow a - 1$
end while
return a

Since half of the elements in $\mathbb{Z}_p^*$ are quadratic residues, a few trials will usually suffice. A more efficient and deterministic approach for the puzzle solver A to generate a quadratic residue from the digest d is the following method:

Algorithm 5 Assigning a unique quadratic residue to the digest d, method 2

Precondition: A (small) quadratic non-residue b modulo p has been found.
if $\left(\frac{d}{p}\right) = 1$ **then** set $a \leftarrow d$
else set $a \leftarrow b \cdot d \bmod p$
return a

According to the properties of the Legendre symbol, the product of two quadratic non-residues is a quadratic residue. Unfortunately, $\left(\frac{1}{p}\right) = 1$ for all p and two other simple candidates for b, namely -1 and 2, also are quadratic residues if $p \equiv 1 \ (mod\ 8)$. Thus, some other (small) number has to be found for b. This can be done in advance for each prime from the list L. Method 2 requires one evaluation of the Legendre symbol and at most one modular multiplication. However, as we will point out in the next subsection, applying the second method makes the verification of the puzzle more expensive compared to the first method.

Now, a unique quadratic residue a has been assigned to A's request. The puzzle to solve is the computation of the square root of a modulo p by applying the Cipolla-Lehmer method, which takes about $2 \cdot log\ p$ sequential modular multiplications. Without parallelization, about $5 \cdot log\ p$ modular multiplications / squarings have to be performed.

Chapter 4 Non-Parallelizable and Non-Interactive Client Puzzles

Having extracted the square root x, host A attaches this n-bit number to its request and sends it to host B. The other square root $-x$ is of no importance for the protocol. There is no need to transmit the prime p. Host A can simply indicate the modulus by stating its position in the list L. Usually, all primes in the list will differ in size so that the corresponding prime may even be deduced from the size of x.

Due to the non-interactive puzzle construction an attacker might compute puzzle solutions in advance. If precomputation is an issue, it can be mitigated by concatenating the message m with an unpredictable, periodically changing number pior to producing the digest d. Lottery results [Bac02] or stock market prices are possible sources of randomness which are easily accessible to both parties A and B. In this case host B will accept only requests bearing an up-to-date random number. In Chapter 5, we will fundamentally solve the precomputation issue of non-interactive client puzzles by deriving the puzzle from a periodically changing random beacon that is broadcasted in the LAN.

4.3.2 Puzzle Verification

The victimized host B verifies the puzzle solution x prior to allocating resources and processing host A's request, which may require to perform a public or even private key operation or an expensive database lookup. Puzzle verification is quite cheap—besides a few hash operations (c times, depends on the hash size and the length of the prime) to compute the digest d from the request only a single modular squaring operation $x^2 \bmod p$ has to be carried out.

If the first method (Algorithm 4) has been applied for assigning a quadratic residue to the digest d, then host B does not need to rerun the algorithm to verify the quadratic residue $a = x^2 \bmod p$ presented by the puzzle solver A. With probability 0.5 we have $a = d$, with probability 0.25 we have $a = d - 1$ and so on. Thus, if $d - (x^2 \bmod p) < \delta$ where δ is a small constant, e. g., $\delta = 20$, the verification can be considered as successful, otherwise A's request is dropped. This check requires only a single modular subtraction and a comparison. Host A cannot take any advantage of extracting the modular square root from $a' = a - \beta$ instead of from a if β is bounded by the small constant δ. Even if host A cheats in this manner for some reason, host B can be certain that A has indeed computed a modular square root specially for its request m. A drawback of the second

4.3 Client Puzzles from Modular Square Roots

method (Algorithm 5) is that the verifier B has to rerun it to ensure that the puzzle solver A has actually extracted the modular square root from the quadratic residue that belongs to the digest d.

Host B's decision whether to allocate resources for processing A's request or not can, of course, also depend on the puzzle difficulty (that is, on the size of the chosen prime) and on the strength of the ongoing DoS attack. The rate of accepted requests with correct puzzle solutions shall not exceed host B's processing capacity, i.e., the rate at which B can actually complete these requests. Being rejected, host A may then retry by taking a larger prime from the list L and solving a more difficult puzzle.

4.3.3 Puzzle Granularity and Public Auditability

The ability to finely adjust the puzzle difficulty to different levels represents an important criterion for the practical applicability of a puzzle. Solving a modular square root puzzle with an N-bit prime takes $\mathcal{O}(N^3)$ time while the verification runs in $\mathcal{O}(N^2)$. Thus, having polynomial granularity, our puzzle is quite fine-grained. In contrast, a non-interactive puzzle scheme based on hash-reversal has exponential granularity and is highly parallelizable. Since a third party can efficiently verify the solution of the square root puzzle without access to any trapdoor information, its cost-function is called *publicly auditable* [Bac02]. Time-lock [RSW96] and Diffie-Hellman based [WJHF04] puzzles are, by contrast, not publicly auditable.

4.3.4 Interactive Client Puzzles

Our modular square root puzzles can be also employed in an interactive way, where the victimized server (host B) issues a challenge to the client (host A), as is the case with client puzzles proposed by Juels and Brainard [JB99] and reworked by Aura et al. [ANL01]. In the interactive setting the prime modulus p and the quadratic residue a are dictated by the server. This can be done in a stateless manner by hashing the client's request along with a secret number to produce the digest d and sending d back to the client, which derives from it the quadratic residue a for the puzzle. Thus, the server needs to store only the secret number and the prime which are reused across all clients. The

Chapter 4 Non-Parallelizable and Non-Interactive Client Puzzles

---

advantages of interactive client puzzles are the prevention of precomputation attacks and the precise choice of the puzzle's level of difficulty since it is prescribed by the defending server. However, a major drawback of interactive client puzzles that we have already indicated in Section 3.1 and in the beginning of this chapter is the lack of authentication for the packet containing the puzzle parameters, which the server sends to the client. A second DoS attack against the clients with faked packets bearing the server's sender address and containing bogus puzzle parameters may thwart the clients' connection attempts. Forging the sender address and eavesdropping on the traffic is an easy matter in wired and especially wireless LANs while it is more difficult in the Internet. Hence, only in environments where counterattacks on the clients are very unlikely, our square root puzzles should be used in the interactive manner.

4.3.5 Client Puzzles from Modular Cube Roots?

We have investigated whether our non-parallelizable and non-interactive client puzzles can be improved by resorting to modular cube roots instead of modular square roots. Obviously, verifying a modular cube root is about twice as expensive since in $x^3 \bmod p$ a modular squaring and a modular multiplication have to be carried out. What about the computation of modular cube roots? Like with modular square roots, the difficulty of solving the congruence $x^3 \equiv a \pmod{p}$ depends on the prime p. If $p \equiv 2 \pmod{3}$ extracting the cube root modulo p is very easy—it requires a single modular inversion and exponentiation [BS96]. The remaining case $p \equiv 1 \pmod{3}$, and especially if $p \equiv 1 \pmod{9}$, is the difficult one [NHSK09]. For $p \equiv 1 \pmod{3}$ one third of the elements in $\mathbb{Z}_p$ are cubic residues. Adleman, Manders, and Miller [AMM77] generalized the Tonelli-Shanks method to compute n-th roots in $\mathbb{Z}_p$. Its running time again depends on the decomposition of $p-1$, in case of cube roots on $p-1 = 3^s t$ where $3 \nmid t$, and is in $\mathcal{O}((\log p)^4)$ in the worst case. In [NHSK09], Nishihara et al. proposed two algorithms to extend the Cipolla-Lehmer method for cube root computation. Its running time is always in $\mathcal{O}((\log p)^3)$ since it ignores the structure of $p-1$. To extract a modular cube root an irreducible monic polynomial f in $\mathbb{Z}_p[x]$ of degree 3 has to be constructed first. This step requires randomization and in case of the more efficient algorithm it takes one modular exponentiation per trial to verify f. The success probability is approximately $\frac{2}{3}$. The actual cube root computation is very similar to the Cipolla-Lehmer method and consists of a single exponentiation in the polynomial ring $\mathbb{Z}_p[x]$:

$$r = x^{(p^2+p+1)/3} \mod f. \quad \text{(Note: } r \text{ will be an integer.)} \tag{4.4}$$

To perform this exponentiation, at least $2 \cdot \log p$ squarings in $\mathbb{Z}_p[x]$ have to be carried out. Squaring a polynomial of degree 2 over the field $\mathbb{Z}_p$ requires 6 modular integer multiplications / squarings. Note that they can be performed in parallel. Reducing the resulting polynomial of degree 4 modulo f by means of a polynomial division takes two sequential steps each one involving 4 modular integer multiplications, which are also parallelizable. Assuming maximal parallelization, this results in at least $6 \cdot \log p$ sequential modular multiplications / squarings on integers to carry out the exponentiation. Taking also the construction of f into account, it requires at least $7 \cdot \log p$ sequential modular multiplications / squarings to solve a modular cube root puzzle versus $2 \cdot \log p$ sequential operations in case of modular square roots. Since the verification of modular cube roots is twice as expensive, the complexity gain with respect to non-parallelizability is about 1.75. We observe that constructing client puzzles from modular cube roots is an interesting option, but it also disproportionately increases the workload for benign hosts which probably solve the puzzle without parallelization.

4.4 Evaluation and Protocol Enhancements

In this section we evaluate the performance of our puzzle scheme and enhance it by introducing a bandwidth-based cost factor for the client.

4.4.1 Puzzle Benchmark

For "hard" primes of different size ranging from 264 to 8206 bits we measure the number of modular square root puzzles that an off-the-shelf Intel Core 2 Quad Q9400 2.66 GHz CPU can verify per second and the time it takes to solve a puzzle. Table 4.1 presents our benchmark results averaged over 10 runs. In all test series the coefficient of variation was below 1.5%. For the large-integer arithmetic we employ the well-known open source library *GMP* from GNU [GMP], which claims to be faster than any other bignum library

Chapter 4 Non-Parallelizable and Non-Interactive Client Puzzles

by using state-of-the-art algorithms with highly optimized assembly code. Modular square root extraction is done using the Cipolla-Lehmer method, where the exponentiation in $\mathbb{Z}_p[x]$ constitutes the main workload. In our measurements we take only the time to perform the $2 \cdot \log p$ sequential modular multiplications into account, since the remaining $3 \cdot \log p$ modular multiplications / squarings can be computed in parallel by a well-versed attacker (see Section 4.2.3). All computations are performed using a single CPU core. For full parallelization of a puzzle an attacker would employ three CPU cores while the defending host can verify as many puzzles in parallel as CPU cores are available. Solving a puzzle on a benign host that uses only a single CPU core actually takes about two and a half times longer than stated in Table 4.1. To accelerate the repeated modular multiplications we make use of Montgomery reduction [Mon85] instead of performing the classical reduction by dividing. This results in a speed-up by a factor of 1.2 – 2.0, especially for small moduli in the order of 264 – 2058 bits.

Table 4.1: Benchmark: verifying and solving modular square root puzzles on Intel Core 2 Quad Q9400 2.66 GHz.

bit length	modular squarings / sec (one CPU core)		modular square root: time in msec (assuming full parallelization)	
	32-bit	64-bit	32-bit	64-bit
264	1 377 000	2 597 000	0.238	0.091
520	593 500	1 354 000	1.35	0.411
776	329 400	698 300	4.15	1.10
1031	201 300	549 400	9.01	2.42
1547	102 500	337 400	27.7	7.09
2058	62 810	199 100	62.9	15.7
3084	33 030	117 100	196	48.1
4106	20 530	71 630	429	109
6155	10 620	39 250	1350	340
8206	6810	24 430	3020	763

Evaluating the benchmark results, we first observe that a 64-bit implementation outperforms its 32-bit counterpart by a factor of up to 3.7 in verifying and up to 4.0 in solving a puzzle. Since almost all desktop CPUs manufactured during the last five years are 64-bit capable and 64-bit operating systems are widely available, we consider the

64-bit results as reference values. Secondly, the speed gap between the verifier and the solver constitutes factor 236 for a 264-bit puzzle and increases up to factor 18 640 for a 8206-bit puzzle. Now the main question to pose is whether the verification throughput of modular square root puzzles is high enough to cope with a DoS flooding attack of bogus puzzle solutions mounted at full link speed. Of course, the size of a valid-looking request containing a puzzle solution plays a role. Before we can definitely answer this question with "yes" for networks with 100 Mbit, 1 Gbit, and even 10 Gbit links, we get back to the central idea of our counter-flooding approach from the previous chapter and extend the puzzle protocol by a small *bandwidth-based cost factor* for the client.

The victimized host demands that valid puzzle solution packets must be padded with zeros to have full MTU size. In the Internet, the MTU usually is 1500 bytes (in Gigabit Ethernet even up to 9000 bytes). Hence, besides solving a puzzle, the client must additionally pay with bytes, i.e., bandwidth becomes a supplementary currency in addition to CPU time. Now, dealing with 1500 byte packets, the victimized host will receive up to 8300 (100 Mbit link), 83 000 (1 Gbit link) or 830 000 (10 Gbit link) valid-looking puzzle solutions per second. We note that it will perfectly cope with 8206-bit puzzles on a 100 Mbit link, with 3084-bit puzzles on a 1 Gbit link and with 520-bit puzzles on a 10 Gbit link assuming a single CPU core engaged in puzzle verification. The time to compute the digest d must also be taken into account. But only the meaningful part of the request and not the whole packet needs to be hashed, while cryptographic hash functions like MD5 or SHA-1 process about 2.8–3.6 Gbit of data per second on our test machine. Furthermore it is conceivable to produce the $(n-1)$-bit digest d by applying a very fast pseudorandom number generator to $H(m)$ instead of executing the hash function c times. On the opposite side it takes an attacker 763 msec to solve a 8206-bit puzzle, 48.1 msec to solve a 3084-bit puzzle, and 0.411 msec to solve a 520-bit puzzle, respectively, assuming full parallelization. Though for modular square root puzzles the level of difficulty cannot be chosen arbitrarily high without rendering the verification too expensive, we are convinced that the presented solution times in the order of 0.1 to 1000 msec are fully viable for DoS prevention in practice. Solution times much greater than 1 second are possible with hash-reversal puzzles, but for benign clients such long delays seem to be hardly reasonable.

Fast modular exponentiation has been also successfully implemented in hardware, especially on *Field-Programmable Gate Arrays (FPGAs)* [CMMDM03, Suz07], and for modern GPUs [Fle07, SG08, HW09], which are very competitive. A few years ago FPGAs outperformed ordinary software implementations, but a current comparison [SG08] shows that nowadays FPGAs are about as fast as software implementations on up-to-date CPUs. A GPU implementation pays off when performing a large number of modular exponentiations simultaneously. However, this comes at the expense of high latency. A speed-up of up to 4 times compared to a modern CPU has been reported in [HW09]. Though an experienced attacker can benefit from such hardware acceleration, his advantage over a regular solver running a software implementation is bounded by a small factor. In general, this is not an issue for the client puzzle protocol.

4.4.2 Increasing the Bandwidth-Based Payment

Besides prescribing that puzzle solution packets must be padded to have full MTU size we may go a step further and increase the bandwidth-based payment requested from the client. The victimized host can demand multiple copies of the puzzle solution packet prior to processing the associated request. This enables us to employ more complex puzzles in high-speed networks and thus to strengthen the DoS protection. For example, by prescribing that clients must send four copies of their puzzle solution packet we can cut down on the number of valid-looking puzzle solutions received per second by factor four and verify even 8206-bit puzzles on a 1 Gbit link. Sending multiple copies of the puzzle solution packet is feasible for all clients regardless of their link speed, while DoS protection schemes based solely on bandwidth payment penalize clients behind slow links. To implement this protocol extension, the victimized host must maintain a packet counter for each client. An appropriate data structure for this purpose is a hash map with the client's address as the key and the pair <*packet counter, timestamp*> as the value. Elements with old timestamps must be purged periodically from the hash map. Storage overhead for maintaining the counters is fairly low: Assuming 10 bytes per client, a 1 Gbit link with 83 000 packets / sec, and a maximum lifetime of 5 sec for each entry, the size of the hash map will be about 10 MB (depending on implementation and pointer size).

4.5 Chapter Summary

In this chapter, we have introduced a novel client puzzle scheme based on modular square roots as a countermeasure against DoS attacks. A modular square root puzzle is non-parallelizable, i.e., the solution cannot be obtained faster than scheduled by distributing the puzzle to multiple machines or CPU cores. Our puzzles can be employed non-interactively, which prevents counterattacks on the client mounted by injecting packets with fake puzzle parameters. Providing polynomial granularity and compact solution and verification functions, modular square root puzzles can be easily implemented to safeguard network protocols, especially those performing expensive public-key authentication, against DoS. We have shown how to raise the efficiency of our puzzle scheme by introducing a bandwidth-based cost factor for the client and demonstrated its feasibility in 1 and 10 Gigabit networks through benchmarking.

In homogeneous LANs, where the link speed of all hosts is equal, counter-flooding from Chapter 3 is without doubt a viable approach to mitigate DoS attacks on public-key handshakes which are performed relatively infrequently. Under weak assumptions it provides bounds to ensure that a benign host will get served. On the other hand our modular square root puzzles seem to be more appropriate when operating in heterogeneous environments with different link speeds. They can be equally applied in LANs, Intranets, and in the Internet to protect various network services.

Chapter 4 Non-Parallelizable and Non-Interactive Client Puzzles

Chapter 5

Secure Client Puzzle Architecture based on Random Beacons

The non-parallelizable and non-interactive client puzzle scheme from the previous chapter was the first step towards a thorough DoS protection in LANs by means of client puzzles. In this chapter, we take the next step. After recapitulating the authentication issue of interactive client puzzles and taking a closer look at it, we introduce a secure architecture that overcomes a considerable drawback of non-interactive puzzles, namely the possibility of precomputing puzzle solutions.

In a counterattack on interactive client puzzles an attacker targets at prospective clients by flooding faked packets that pretend to come from the defending server and contain bogus puzzle parameters. The feasibility of such a counterattack depends on the network environment and the attacker's location. Forging the sender address is especially easy in wired and wireless LANs while it is more difficult in the Internet. The capability to eavesdrop on the traffic, which is a simple matter in WiFi networks, facilitates the attack but is not a necessary condition. An attacker who cannot overhear the client's request may continuously inject faked puzzle challenges. This proactive counterattack would take effect when the client actually issues a request. A client receiving a plethora of bogus challenges that were possibly chosen to be even more difficult than the puzzle of the genuine server may easily become overwhelmed. Most likely, it would not be able to solve the authentic challenge and thus its request would not be processed by the server. Depending on the chosen puzzle strength, even a modest puzzle packet rate may be sufficient for the attacker to succeed. Authenticating the challenge packet by means of a digital signature is not an option, since its generation and even verification are too expensive to be performed for all incoming requests[1]. For that very reason network protocols that employ public-key cryptography may be vulnerable to DoS and should be protected by means of client puzzles.

We tackle the problem of authentication for client puzzles by introducing a secure architecture where clients construct and solve *non-interactive* puzzles from a *random beacon*. The main idea is to employ client puzzles non-interactively, which eliminates authentication issues with the server's challenge message, and to prevent precomputation of puzzle solutions by deriving puzzles from a periodically changing, secure random beacon. The beacons are generated in advance for a longer time span and are broadcasted in the LAN by a special beacon server. All hosts obtain a signed fingerprint package consisting of cryptographic digests of these beacons. Verifying a beacon is very easy—it takes only a single hash operation, which can be performed at line speed by all hosts. Thus, DoS attacks on the beacon service are virtually impossible. If a server becomes overloaded due to a DoS attack, it asks all clients to solve and submit a puzzle prior to processing their requests. A client constructs a non-interactive puzzle by taking its request and the current beacon as input for a cost function. This can be, e.g., the reversal of a one-way hash function by brute force or the computation of a modular square root. Having solved the puzzle, the client attaches the puzzle parameters and the solution to the pending request and retransmits it.

Our major contribution in this chapter lies in the development of sophisticated techniques to provide a robust and secure beacon service. We address synchronization aspects and especially elaborate the deployment of beacon fingerprints. Even if hosts were not able to obtain the signed fingerprint package using one of the regular distribution channels, they can acquire it on the fly from the beacon server and verify its signature despite of possible DoS flooding attacks. Our client puzzle architecture is primarily designed for LANs. But we show how to adopt the beacon service to operate with a single beacon server in Intranets or even in the Internet. This chapter is based on a paper that has been accepted for publication [JM12b].

---

[1]Example calculation: A current desktop machine can verify roughly 1000–3000 DSA-1024 signatures or 10 000–35 000 RSA-1024 signatures per second while on a 1 Gbit link an attacker can flood up to 83 333 full MTU (1500 bytes) packets containing bogus signatures. If we assume smaller packet sizes the load induced by the attacker would be even higher.

The remainder of the chapter is structured as follows. In the next section, we briefly look at some existing client puzzle architectures. Section 5.2 presents our secure client puzzle architecture, describes the construction of puzzles from a periodically changing random beacon and details how to deploy and verify these beacons. In Section 5.3, we extend our scheme by providing techniques to deliver beacons across LAN boundaries and by introducing a service which enables emergency deployment of signed beacon fingerprints. Finally, in Section 5.4, we conclude this chapter by summarizing the main results.

5.1 Related Work

In Section 4.1, we have already discussed various client puzzle schemes proposed in the literature. In this section, we highlight the architectural aspects of three previous works on client puzzles.

Wang and Reiter [WR08] proposed a multi-layer framework for puzzle-based DoS defense, which embeds puzzle techniques into both IP-layer and end-to-end services. The authors have presented two mechanisms: *Congestion puzzles* address bandwidth-exhaustion attacks in routers by cooperatively imposing puzzles to clients whose traffic is traversing a congested link. A traffic flow must be accompanied by a corresponding computation flow of puzzle solutions. The second mechanism called *puzzle auctions* protects an end-to-end service like TCP against protocol-specific DoS attacks. Clients bid for server resources by tuning the difficulty of the hash-reversal puzzle that they solve and the server allocates its limited resources to the highest bidder first.

In the client puzzle architecture suggested by Waters et al. [WJHF04] puzzle construction and distribution are outsourced to a secure entity called bastion (see Section 4.1). But as with Juels' client puzzles, the secure distribution of puzzle challenges to the clients remains an open issue also in Waters' scheme. The authors touch on the possibility of deriving puzzles from the emissions of a random beacon and state hashes of financial-market data or Internet news as candidates for a mutual source of randomness. But authentication of the input data is again an unsolved problem, especially in environments that do not enforce address authenticity. By injecting packets with faked data or beacons an attacker might render the DoS protection useless. With Waters we share the general idea of constructing puzzles from a random beacon and develop an architecture for a secure, real-world random beacon service. Our main contribution is a solid solution to the authentication problem that we tackle from scratch and thus rule out counterattacks on the puzzle distribution.

Feng et al. implemented *network puzzles* at the "weakest link"—the IP layer—to make them universally usable [FKFL05]. Network puzzles can be selectively applied to different communication channels established by a client. By introducing hint-based hash-reversal puzzles the authors achieved linear granularity for interactive hash-reversal puzzles (see Section 4.1). The feasibility of the puzzle protocol has been demonstrated through an implementation on Linux with *iptables*. The authors use ICMP source quench messages to deliver puzzles and IP options to transmit client cookies and puzzle answers. However, their protocol is based on the assumption that the attacker cannot read or modify any packets sent between the client and the server. In contrast, we assume that the attacker is able to eavesdrop on the traffic.

5.2 Secure Client Puzzle Architecture

Our attack model assumes an adversary (or a group of adversaries) that can inject arbitrary packets and, in particular, spoof the sender's IP and MAC address. The attacker may also be capable to eavesdrop on some or even all packets sent by the legitimate hosts. However, he has only a very limited capability to modify packets or to destroy them by causing packet losses in switches or in the medium. Otherwise the attacker could render communication impossible simply by corrupting the data or through destruction of whole packets. Against such a threat puzzles would be of no avail.

5.2.1 Non-Interactive Client Puzzles

We suggest employing client puzzles in a *non-interactive* way where the client constructs the puzzle, solves it and attaches the solution to its request. To avoid the waste of time and CPU resources during normal operation when the server is not suffering from a DoS

5.2 Secure Client Puzzle Architecture

attack the client first sends its request without a puzzle solution. If the server replies in the regular manner everything is fine. In case of a DoS attack the server responds with a DoS alert message and drops the client's request without processing it further. The DoS alert message is an indication to the client that it must solve a puzzle prior to being served. Of course this message might be also a fake and currently there is no overload condition at the server. However, an unnecessarily solved puzzle is harmless and the client can cope with wrong alerts by introducing a timeout. A DoS alert message is considered authentic if no regular response has been received from the server during a certain time period. Now the client constructs a puzzle, solves it and retransmits its request along with the puzzle parameters and solution in a single message. The first time the client chooses for its puzzle the default level of difficulty, which has to be specified for the protocol or service that is safeguarded from DoS by client puzzles. A required solution time of 50–200 milliseconds on a single CPU core of an off-the-shelf desktop machine may be a reasonable value. If the server does not respond the DoS attack may be stronger than expected. The client should retry after a timeout by doubling the initial puzzle difficulty, solving a more complex puzzle and retransmitting its request in combination with the new proof of work. Several connection attempts with an exponentially growing puzzle difficulty should be carried out prior to giving up.

During an overload condition the server must parse all incoming requests, answer with a DoS alert message and verify all submitted puzzle solutions. Its computing power must be chosen high enough to perform this puzzle preprocessing at full bandwidth and to serve requests at an ordinary rate without becoming overburdened. Only requests from clients that have solved a puzzle and submitted a correct solution have a chance of being processed. A priority queue can be used to manage requests carrying puzzles with different levels of difficulty. The request from the client that has solved the most difficult puzzle is served fist. To limit the queue size a periodic cleanup should purge requests that have stayed in the queue longer than a predefined time interval.

5.2.2 Client Puzzles from a Random Beacon

We should prevent the reuse of a single puzzle solution by multiple different requests without demanding from the server to log spent puzzles solutions. This can be achieved

Chapter 5 Secure Client Puzzle Architecture based on Random Beacons

by binding the puzzle to the request so that a different request requires solving a completely new puzzle. In our client puzzle architecture a cryptographic digest of the request must flow into the puzzle construction. Nevertheless the protocol or service running on the server must provide some mechanism to recognize identical requests originating from the same client so that resources (e.g., database lookup or signature verification / computation) required to complete such requests are committed only once.

A serious issue with non-interactive client puzzles may pose precomputation attacks where the attacker prepares a huge pile of requests and corresponding puzzle solutions in advance. He might engage dozens of machines, e.g., from a botnet, to solve thousands of puzzles which enables him to overwhelm a server by flooding his prepared requests at some point in the future. We address this threat by constructing client puzzles from a periodically changing random beacon. The beacon is broadcasted in the whole network at regular intervals so that both client and server have access to a mutual source of randomness. This renders precomputation attacks virtually impossible since the beacon is unpredictable and puzzles derived from it are valid only for a short period of time.

Combining these two ideas we create our client puzzles from the cryptographic digest of the request r and the current random beacon b. Let H be a cryptographic hash function (e.g., SHA-1 or RIPEMD-160), then the input for the puzzle construction is the d-bit digest

$$s = H(r \mid\mid b) \tag{5.1}$$

where $\mid\mid$ denotes the concatenation of two bit strings.

5.2.3 Puzzle Construction

Our client puzzle architecture does not depend on a specific cost function. The only requirement is that the puzzle can be derived *by the client* from an arbitrary number, which is the digest s in our scenario. In case of the well-known hash-reversal cost function [JB99, Bac02, ANL01] the puzzle is to find by brute force a bit string x so that

$$H(s \mid\mid x) = \underbrace{0\,0\,0 \ldots 0\,0\,0}_{\substack{\text{first } q \text{ bits} \\ \text{are zero}}} \underbrace{Z}_{\substack{\text{remaining} \\ d-q \text{ bits}}} \tag{5.2}$$

5.2 Secure Client Puzzle Architecture

To simplify the implementation x should be a fixed-length integer (e.g., 64 bits), which is initialized with zero and incremented by one for each new try. The number of leading zero bits q in the output of H determines the puzzle difficulty. Increasing q by one doubles each time the expected number of tries to find a suitable x. Thus, the granularity of the hash-reversal puzzle is exponential.

In the previous chapter, we have designed a novel non-interactive client puzzle scheme that is based on the computation of square roots modulo a prime. Solving a modular square root puzzle involves several modular exponentiations whereas verification requires performing only a single modular squaring operation. While a hash-reversal puzzle can be solved in parallel by multiple machines or CPU cores and has only exponential granularity, a modular square root puzzle is non-parallelizable to a high degree and provides polynomial granularity. Moreover, the solution time of a hash-reversal puzzle is highly nondeterministic, while a modular square root puzzle has only a negligible probabilistic component[2]. A minor drawback of modular square root puzzles is that the level of difficulty cannot be chosen arbitrarily high without rendering verification too expensive. The size of the solution also grows with increasing puzzle difficulty. But for solution times which are usually chosen in the order of milliseconds modular square root puzzles are acceptably small, can be verified at line speed, and hence are fully viable for DoS prevention in practice. For our secure client puzzle architecture they might thus be even better candidates than hash-reversal puzzles.

5.2.4 Random Beacon Server

The random beacon server B is ideally a dedicated machine in the LAN that periodically broadcasts a beacon packet containing a n-bit random number b. Depending on the layer at which client puzzles are employed, the beacon message is encapsulated in a raw Ethernet frame, an IP datagram or in a UDP segment. To render any network-based attacks on the beacon server impossible, we suggest to disable the receiver unit of B's network interface or simply to drop all incoming packets without inspecting them. Only outgoing packets to provide the beacon service should be permitted. An isolated beacon

---
[2]This is the search for a quadratic non-residue modulo p in the Cipolla-Lehmer method. By taking primes $p \equiv 3 \pmod 4$ and relaxing the puzzle complexity to a single modular exponentiation (see Equation 4.1 on page 55) the puzzle could be made completely deterministic.

server that does not receive any input is DoS-resistant by design. The requirement of setting up a dedicated machine may be of course relaxed at the expense of security. Basically, any existing server in the LAN can run the beacon service. Since the computational burden is minimal, even an off-the-shelf desktop machine would suffice for this task. Thus, setting up a beacon server does not constitute a demanding infrastructure requirement.

The random numbers to be included in the beacons are generated in advance for a time span of several days, weeks, or even months. In practice, this task can be accomplished by a cryptographically secure pseudorandom number generator that runs on the beacon server. For the generation of a set of random numbers three parameters have to be provided: the bit length n of each number, the time span t covered by the set, and the beacon period p, i.e., the time between the emission of the current and the next random number. In practice, t and p will be measured in seconds. The set consists of $k = \frac{t}{p}$ random numbers requiring $k \cdot n$ bits of output from the random number generator.

Next, for each random number b_i, $1 \leq i \leq k$, we compute a d-bit digest $H(b_i)$ by applying the cryptographic hash function H. These are the *fingerprints* of the random beacons. Now a *fingerprint package* $<T_{Start}, t, p, H(b_1), ..., H(b_k)>$ is created and digitally signed using the private key of the beacon server B. T_{Start} is a timestamp that denotes the time when the emission of the associated beacons starts. We expect that the beacon server has obtained a public-key certificate from a well-known certificate authority and that everyone can verify its signature on the fingerprint package if B's certificate is attached. The final step is the deployment of the signed fingerprint package to all hosts in the network that will either solve or verify client puzzles in case of a DoS attack. The preferable method is to publish the signed fingerprint package along with B's certificate on the institution's website, where it can be downloaded and verified by all users or hosts. A manual deployment by sending the fingerprints via e-mail or obtaining them on a USB flash drive from the network administrator may be also conceivable in some scenarios. Instead of contacting the network administrator one could also imagine to install a physically secured terminal somewhere in the building where users can store the fingerprint package on their USB flash drive by themselves. The size of the fingerprint package depends on the covered time span t and the beacon period p, but is reasonably small even for long time spans and short intervals. For example, for $t = 30\ days$ and $p = 60\ sec$ we need $k = 43\,200$ fingerprints, which occupy about 844 KB if using SHA-1 with a digest length d of 160 bits.

At time T_{Start} the beacon server switches to the new beacon set by emitting the random number b_1 which is valid until $T_{Start} + p$. Every p seconds the current number b_i is replaced by releasing its successor b_{i+1}. Since broadcast transmissions are not reliable, a beacon packet may get lost. Therefore we propose to periodically retransmit the current beacon during its lifetime, e. g., to broadcast it once a second. This ensures that all hosts in the network, even those that have joined recently, will receive the current beacon without noticeable delay. An appropriate bit length n for random numbers to generate client puzzles that are unpredictable is in the order of a cryptographic hash, e. g., 160–256 bits. Hence, beacon packets are very small, no more than 60–70 bytes including all protocol headers (e. g., UDP, IP, and Ethernet).

5.2.5 Receiving and Verifying the Beacons

All clients and servers (in the following just called hosts) in the network obtain the fingerprint package in advance using one of the deployment techniques described in the previous subsection. We assume that the clocks of all hosts and the beacon server are loosely synchronized. The allowable time skew δ may be in order of minutes. This requirement can be easily achieved even without a time synchronization protocol like NTP [Mil92], just by letting the users manually adjust their computer's clock occasionally. To synchronize with the beacon server a host begins at time $T_{Start} - \delta$ to verify all incoming beacon packets by computing the beacon's digest and matching it against $H(b_1)$ from the fingerprint package. Having received a beacon b with $H(b) = H(b_1)$ the host records the beginning of the new beacon period and sets b_1 a the current beacon. This synchronization will succeed at the latest at time $T_{Start} + \delta$. Subsequent beacons that the host receives are matched against $H(b_2)$, or to generalize, after having verified and set b_i the host matches new beacons against $H(b_{i+1})$ and switches to b_{i+1} if the comparison succeeds.

Hosts that join the network during a beacon period can also synchronize with the beacon server in a straightforward manner. A host joining at time $T_{Start} + h$ (according to its clock) matches incoming beacons against a list L of fingerprints, namely

$L = \langle H(b_{v-r}), ..., H(b_{v+r+2}) \rangle$ with $v = \lceil \frac{h}{p} \rceil$ and $r = \lceil \frac{\delta}{p} \rceil$. In case of a match with one of the fingerprints from the list the beacon b is set as the tentative beacon and all fingerprints preceding it in the list are removed. The host continues to verify subsequent beacons for $2p$ seconds. This ensures that it definitely hits and observes a complete beacon period. If a subsequent beacon corresponds to a newer fingerprint from the list, then it becomes the tentative beacon and old fingerprints are once again purged from L. This is done to prevent replay attacks with outdated beacons. After $2p$ seconds the synchronization is completed. The tentative beacon becomes the current beacon—now it has definitely been identified.

An attacker may try to interfere with the beacon service by flooding thousands of faked beacon packets bearing the beacon server's sender address. However, computing the cryptographic hash of a packet and matching this digest against a stored value or a small set of values is a cheap task that in general can be performed at full link speed in Gigabit networks. Table 5.1 shows benchmark results of four cryptographic hash functions that we have measured on an Intel Core 2 Quad Q9400 2.66 GHz CPU using a 64-bit Linux distribution, *GCC 4.4* and the cryptographic library *Botan* [Llo]. A single CPU core achieves a throughput of 227–426 MB/sec while a Gigabit link has a transfer rate of 119 MB/sec. Thus, by flooding bogus beacons the attacker is only able to raise the CPU load on the hosts, but cannot prevent the identification of the authentic beacon.

Table 5.1: Benchmark: throughput of cryptographic hash functions on Intel Core 2 Quad Q9400 2.66 GHz (one core active).

hash function	block size	digest length	speed
MD5	512 bits	128 bits	**426.4 MB/s**
RIPEMD-160	512 bits	160 bits	**260.5 MB/s**
SHA-1	512 bits	512 bits	**327.0 MB/s**
SHA-384	1024 bits	384 bits	**227.4 MB/s**

Though beacon packets are periodically retransmitted during a beacon period, a host should not except that it will receive all consecutive beacons. Due to abnormal operation it might sometimes miss some beacons. To recover from this condition we introduce a lookahead of a few fingerprints. Having failed to replace the current beacon b_i by its successor for more than p seconds, the host matches incoming beacons against the next l

fingerprints $H(b_{i+1})$, ..., $H(b_{i+l})$. If the verification still fails for several beacon periods, the host should increase l and, even if this is of no avail, it should adjust i according to the time that has passed since the last beacon update.

5.2.6 Puzzle Submission and Verification

In case of a DoS attack on the server the client submits along with its request r the puzzle solution and the beacon b from which the puzzle has been derived. Instead of transmitting the beacon it can also indicate its index in the fingerprint package. While the client was solving the puzzle or while it stayed in the server's input queue the current beacon may already have changed. Therefore the server must accept also puzzle solutions that were derived from older beacons within reasonable bounds. Considering the proposed puzzle solution time of about 50–200 milliseconds and a beacon period in the order of some seconds we recommend to tolerate only puzzles constructed from the current or the previous beacon. This keeps the protocol simple and effectively prevents precomputation attacks. Requests bearing a puzzle from an outdated beacon are dropped without verification. In networks encountering large delays the beacon period should be chosen accordingly. In case of a valid beacon the server first computes the digest $s = H(r \parallel b)$ and then verifies the solution of the puzzle constructed from s.

5.3 Protocol Extensions

5.3.1 Beacon Distribution across LAN Boundaries

Our secure client puzzle architecture primarily focuses on LANs where counterattacks on interactive client puzzle protocols through injection of bogus challenges are especially easy and thus very promising. But depending on the attacker's power and resources a counterattack with faked puzzle challenges may succeed also in large-scale networks like corporate Intranets or even in the Internet. Especially hosts in the edge network might be vulnerable to puzzle counterattacks. Thus, it can make sense to employ non-interactive client puzzles that are derived from a random beacon also in these settings. However, broadcasting beacons works only within a LAN. A beacon server that shall

Chapter 5 Secure Client Puzzle Architecture based on Random Beacons

supply hosts spread across LAN boundaries with beacons must resort to a different distribution technique. A well-known solution for this task is multicast. Hosts employing the secure client puzzle architecture could subscribe to the multicast group to which the beacon server addresses its periodic beacons. But a major issue with beacon dissemination through multicast is that many ISPs do not route multicast traffic which breaks traditional input-rate-based billing models. Thus, while multicast may be an option for corporate networks administered by a single entity, we must resort to a different approach to provide the beacon service over the Internet.

We propose to deploy beacons across LAN boundaries via unicast and pay particular attention to DoS resilience of the beacon server. Hosts receive the current beacon from the beacon server *on demand* after having issued a corresponding request. Unicast deployment of beacons on a subscription basis where a host issues a single request and hereon periodically receives beacons from the server until it cancels this subscription would be prone to a DoS attack. The attacker could take on many different identities and spawn a multitude of faked subscriptions that might quickly exhaust the bandwidth of the beacon server. Therefore each new beacon that a host receives must be triggered by a separate request. This is a kind of tit-for-tat strategy. The server supplies only those hosts with beacons that themselves spend bandwidth and continuously send corresponding requests. The size of the request packet (usually, a UDP datagram encapsulated in IP) must be at least as large as the beacon packet. To enforce its resistance to DoS the beacon server may even demand that valid beacon requests have to be padded with zeros to have full MTU size, which usually is 1500 bytes (20–25 times larger than the beacon packet). This will raise the costs on the attacker's side and make his attempts to exhaust the server's resources quite useless. On the other side, legitimate hosts requesting every few seconds a new beacon will perfectly cope with this small *bandwidth-based payment* for the beacon service. In Section 4.4.1, we have already applied this strategy to strengthen our client puzzle scheme based on modular square roots. The processing time for a beacon request is minimal. The server performs virtually no computation—it only crafts and sends a reply packet containing the current beacon. Nevertheless, the server capacity, especially its processor and network link, has to be carefully chosen to withstand a fluctuating number of requests including potential attackers. In contrast to the Internet scenario, the broadcast service in a LAN can be

5.3 Protocol Extensions

provided by any off-the-shelf desktop machine.

Requesting a beacon from a beacon server in the Internet is in some respects comparable to a DNS lookup. Indeed, another approach to deploy beacons is to rely on DNS. The beacon server becomes the authoritative name server for a particular domain. Hosts receive the current beacon by requesting a TXT resource record. In its reply the beacon server must set the TTL to a value smaller than the beacon period p. Choosing $\frac{p}{2}$ for the TTL seems to be appropriate to guarantee freshness and at the same time to distribute load. Owing to DNS caching the number of requests going end-to-end from host to beacon server will be significantly cut down which results in a smaller traffic footprint.

5.3.2 Emergency Deployment of Beacon Fingerprints

Obtaining the signed fingerprint package is a crucial step in the setup of our secure client puzzle architecture. In the previous section we have proposed several deployment techniques (download from a website, manual distribution via e-mail or USB flash drive, secure terminal) to achieve this goal. However, an attacker may try to sabotage the download of the fingerprints by mounting a DoS attack against the web server or through injection of spoofed packets, e.g, TCP resets, aiming to impede the connection. Secure transmission via SSL or IPSec does not protect from DoS attacks, since these protocols rely on expensive public-key cryptography and themselves may require protection from DoS by means of client puzzles. Manual distribution of the fingerprint package can be too expensive in large networks while some institutions might not be able to afford the installation of a secure terminal. Therefore we introduce a further deployment method for the fingerprints as a fallback option for emergency situations, where the other distribution channels fail. It is designed to work within a LAN.

Resorting to the Beacon Server

The beacon server can periodically broadcast the current fingerprint package by dividing it into several packets. If the current fingerprint package covers a very long time span resulting in a large number of packets, the beacon server builds a smaller one which contains only the beacons for the next few hours or days. Assume that it takes g packets to deliver the fingerprint package which must be also digitally signed. To enable an efficient verification of each of the g packets for the receiver the beacon server computes the cryptographic hash of each packet and signs a list consisting of these g digests plus the timestamp T_{Start}. The digest list along with the timestamp and the signature must fit into a single packet—the header of the fingerprint package. Thus, g is bounded by the MTU, the signature size and the digest length d. Assuming 1500 bytes for the first, 1024 bits for the second and 160 bits for the third factor we obtain $g \leq 68$. The beacon server periodically broadcasts the header packet followed by the g numbered fingerprint packets. A host requiring the fingerprint package first waits for the header packet, verifies its signature and timestamp and stores the g digests of the fingerprint packets. Now it is ready to receive and quickly validate the fingerprint packets by computing their digest and matching this digest against the list. The order of the received fingerprint packets is irrelevant since each packet has a sequence number and can be independently verified and stored. Having collected all g parts of the fingerprint package the host finally needs to synchronize with the beacon server to identify the current beacon.

Fending off Flooding Attacks with Faked Signatures

The deployment of beacon fingerprints by the beacon server is very robust to DoS attacks since the beacon server does not receive any requests and thus cannot be compromised or even influenced from outside. Spoofed fingerprint packets are also harmless—they can be easily detected by checking their digest. The only sticking point is the expensive verification of the signature in the header packet. But we introduce two measures to cope with a potential flooding attack of faked header packets.

The first measure is an *observe-then-verify strategy*. The genuine header packet is periodically retransmitted by the beacon server. Hence only those header packets that a host receives over and over again are potentially authentic and need to be taken into account for verification. Instead of trying to verify all incoming header packets a host first observes the header packets that it receives for some consecutive periods and records them (or their hash values to save memory). After this observation phase only those header packets are selected for verification that have been received repeatedly during multiple periods. Now this pile of header packets gets verified until the genuine signature is found. Checking the included timestamp safeguards against replay attacks. New header packets arriving during this phase are ignored. If all packets from the pile turn out to be faked, a host retries by initiating a new observation phase. The shorter we choose the retransmission period for the header packet, the smaller will be the pile of collected packets that need to be validated and the faster a host will identify the genuine header packet. A retransmission period of 50 msec may be reasonable for the header packet while fingerprint packets are retransmitted, e.g., only every 5 seconds. Assuming a 1 Gbit link, full MTU packets (1500 bytes, this can be enforced by policy), an observation phase taking 1 second (20 periods) and a quota of 0.5 packets per period on average (i.e., at least 10 copies), there will be at most 8333 candidates that must be verified. In case of an RSA-1024 signature having a verification throughput of 10 000 – 35 000 operations per second on current desktop machines it will take less than a second to validate the whole pile of header packets. This sample calculation confirms that the observe-then-verify strategy provides a viable way to quickly filter out the genuine header packet and to obtain the fingerprint package. An alternative, more basic approach which does not require to count duplicates is to collect all header packets arriving during 2 – 4 periods (at most 8333 – 16 666 packets in our example) and then to verify all them. If not too many bursty packet losses occur, at least one genuine header packet will be among this capture with very high probability.

The second measure is optional and aims to significantly cut down the number of valid-looking header packets that the attacker can emit by including a hash-reversal puzzle. Since the beacon server is ideally a dedicated machine which fulfills no other tasks besides broadcasting beacons and fingerprint packages, it has plenty of idle CPU time. This time can be used to solve a hash-reversal puzzle (see Section 5.2.3) for the header packet that will be broadcasted when the next fingerprint package takes effect. The puzzle is derived from the digest of the header packet. The beacon server continues to solve the puzzle by finding new solutions x that yield a larger number q of leading zero bits in the output of H than the previous solution until it is time to deploy the corresponding fingerprint package. For example, if fingerprint packages are issued for 24 hours, the beacon server has 24 hours to solve the puzzle for the corresponding header packet. Due to the nondeterministic nature of the hash-reversal puzzle the puzzle difficulty determined by q will slightly vary from run to run. Hosts waiting for the header packet can drop all packets that have no puzzle attached, carry a wrong solution, or whose puzzle difficulty falls below a predefined threshold. Header packets that have passed this filter are inserted into a priority queue. The packet with the puzzle that has the highest level of difficulty is verified first.

To verify a signature issued by the beacon server B a host requires B's certificate. If it has not cached this certificate in the past when obtaining the fingerprint package along with B's certificate through regular distribution channels, we must provide a way to acquire it on the fly. This can be accomplished in the same manner as the deployment of the signed header packet. The beacon server periodically broadcasts its certificate in a special certificate packet. To withstand a DoS flooding attack with forged certificate packets a host applies the observe-then-verify strategy, which enables to quickly identify and verify the genuine certificate. In addition, the authentic certificate packet may also be protected by a hash-reversal puzzle.

5.4 Chapter Summary

In this chapter, we have presented a secure client puzzle architecture for DoS prevention where puzzles are constructed by the client from a periodic random beacon. By employing client puzzles non-interactively we bypass authentication issues with the challenge message sent from server to client in interactive client puzzle schemes. To rule out pre-computation attacks, valid puzzles must be derived from the current beacon which is broadcasted by the beacon server. Hosts obtain in advance a signed fingerprint package with cryptographic digests of the beacons which enables them to instantly authenticate all incoming beacon packets. We have proposed several regular distribution channels for the fingerprint package and introduced an emergency deployment technique to acquire the beacon fingerprints on the fly from the beacon server. Our beacon service is by design robust against DoS counterattacks. It can operate not only in LANs but also across LAN boundaries by distributing beacons via multicast, unicast, or through DNS.

The secure client puzzle architecture fundamentally solves the precomputation issue of non-interactive client puzzles and can be perfectly coupled with and benefit from

5.4 Chapter Summary

our non-parallelizable modular square root puzzles introduced in the previous chapter. With regard to our cryptographic link layer from Chapter 2, we are convinced that both counter-flooding and the secure client puzzle architecture constitute viable approaches to protect the public-key handshake of CLL against DoS.

Chapter 6

Offline Submission with RSA Time-Lock Puzzles

The application of computational puzzles is not limited to mitigation of DoS attacks. In Section 4.1, we have touched on some other domains that benefit from puzzles and timed-release cryptography is likely the most prominent one. Having developed several protocols and techniques to secure local area networks and to protect them against DoS in the previous four chapters of this thesis, we now present our final contribution, which is in the area of timed-release cryptography. This chapter introduces a novel application for cryptographic puzzles. It deals with offline submission. Not surprisingly, a successful DoS attack may be one of the reasons for disconnectivity and resorting to our offline submission protocol is a potential solution for this emergency scenario.

Online submission of documents like conference papers, homework assignments, applications or claims has become very popular recently. Many institutions even establish paperless electronic submissions as the only submission mode, since it significantly reduces their processing costs. Each call for submission has, of course, its deadline and each document received past the time limit has to be rejected by the institution for fairness reasons. However, there may be situations where the document is completed in time, but cannot be submitted by the author before the expiration of the deadline because of technical issues. One possible reason may be a broken network connection in all its flavors, e.g., the access network—be it ADSL, UMTS, WiFi or dialup—becoming temporarily unavailable, an ISP failure or a DNS resolution problem. The submission

Chapter 6 Offline Submission with RSA Time-Lock Puzzles

server itself may also become temporarily unreachable due to a crash or, as already indicated, due to a DoS attack. Finally, it is also conceivable that by the time of the deadline the author stays in a remote region without Internet access and therefore cannot submit the document in time. Today, in all these scenarios the author just has bad luck and there is nothing he can do about it, since the institution accepting the document is usually not able to verify and thus to consider any mitigating circumstances.

In this chapter, we propose a new cryptographic protocol inspired by Rivest's *time-lock puzzles* [RSW96]. It enables an author to commit to a document in an offline manner before the deadline and to submit it at some time past the deadline when being online again. The main idea is to let the author solve a modular exponentiation puzzle involving an arbitrary large number of *non-parallelizable* modular squaring operations. In Chapter 4, our modular square root puzzles designed for DoS prevention also relied on the non-parallelizability of repeated squaring. We construct the puzzle from the document's cryptographic hash value. The number of puzzle operations is determined by the time period between the deadline and the point in time where the author regains connectivity to the submission server. Each puzzle operation has a time value of some nanoseconds assigned by the institution managing the submission process and is dictated by current CPU speeds. By submitting his document along with the appropriate puzzle solution the author can prove to the institution that the document has actually been completed at some time in the past before the deadline.

We introduce a time-lock RSA puzzle scheme for delayed encryption and signature verification. The basis of our offline submission protocol is a delayed RSA encryption of the document to be submitted using the institution's public key. Having received the delayed submission, the institution verifies the puzzle solution and the assigned level of difficulty by performing an RSA decryption with its private key. Running the offline submission protocol requires the author to hold a computer with a reasonably up-to-date processor and to continuously solve the puzzle from the expiration of the deadline until the actual online submission. Owners of older hardware can compensate by completing the document and beginning to solve the puzzle at some point before the actual deadline—the earlier the better. We show that in combination with the non-parallelizability feature the difference in puzzle processing speed between recent off-the-shelf computers usually does not exceed factor 1.5.

We have implemented a platform-independent tool which performs all parts of our offline submission protocol: puzzle benchmark, issuing a time-lock RSA certificate, solving a puzzle and finally verifying the solution for a submitted document. The tool is available for free download including the sources and can be instantly used by the two parties—institution and author—to enable a delayed submission for an online submission system. To demonstrate the usability of our scheme, we have also set up a Web submission system for homework assignments, which employs our offline submission protocol and makes delayed submission possible. A paper covering the central results of this chapter has been published in [JM10].

The rest of the chapter is organized as follows. In the next section, we review existing approaches to time-lock cryptography. Section 6.2 introduces our RSA time-lock puzzle scheme. In Section 6.3 we describe how to construct an offline submission protocol on that basis. Section 6.4 presents the implementation of our offline submission tool and evaluates its performance. Finally, we conclude this chapter with a summary in Section 6.5.

6.1 Related Work

6.1.1 Time-Lock Puzzles

Time-lock puzzles have been introduced by Rivest et al. [RSW96] to encrypt messages which can be decrypted by others only after a pre-determined amount of time has passed. Possible applications proposed for timed-release cryptography are: sealing bids in an auction which cannot be opened prior the end of the bidding period, releasing documents like diaries in the future, scheduling electronic payments, or implementing a key-escrow scheme where the government can get a secret key after a fixed period. Non-parallelizability of the underlying repeated squaring operation makes up the key feature of time-lock puzzles—the solver cannot speed-up the computation by engaging multiple CPU cores or machines. Rivest's time-lock puzzle is in a way related to his RSA cryptosystem and works as follows: To encrypt a message m for a period of T seconds Alice

Chapter 6 Offline Submission with RSA Time-Lock Puzzles

- generates at random two large primes p and q.
- computes the modulus $n = pq$ and Euler's totient function $\varphi(n) = (p-1)(q-1)$.
- determines the number of squaring operations modulo n per second, denoted by S, that can be performed by the solver Bob, and computes $t = T \cdot S$.
- encrypts m with a symmetric cipher using the key K.
- picks a random a, $1 < a < n$, and encrypts K as

$$C_K = K + a^{2^t} \bmod n. \qquad (6.1)$$

To make the exponentiation efficient, Alice reduces the exponent modulo $\varphi(n)$ by computing

$$r = 2^t \bmod \varphi(n) \qquad (6.2)$$

and obtains $a^{2^t} \bmod n$ from $a^r \bmod n$.

- outputs the time-lock puzzle (n, a, t, C_K).

To reveal K from C_K, Bob needs to compute $a^{2^t} \bmod n$ and in contrast to Alice cannot take the shortcut via $\varphi(n)$, since determining $\varphi(n)$ is provably as hard as factoring n. Instead, Bob must do the computation step by step by repeatedly performing modular squarings—altogether t times which takes T seconds. As we have pointed out in Section 4.2.3, this is assumed to be an intrinsically sequential process, but it is still an open question whether modular exponentiation is P-complete, i.e., not in NC. Likewise, it is unknown if factoring is really not in P. Hence, the security of time-lock puzzles is based on these two unproven assumptions. They are considered to be hard and important problems for many years.

A comprehensive survey on efficient algorithms for modular exponentiation can be found in [MvOV96] and [Gor98]. The most important algorithms beside the basic binary exponentiation are the k-ary method, the sliding-window method, and addition chains. However, when dealing with a power-of-two exponent as is the case with time-lock puzzles, repeated squaring—a special case of the binary exponentiation—constitutes the most efficient technique. To compute $a^x \bmod n$ with $x = 2^t$ it takes t modular squarings and no additional multiplications while $\lfloor \log x \rfloor$ is the lower bound for the number of multiplications to perform a single exponentiation in a general group. To accelerate the modular multiplication, especially when being performed repeatedly during modular exponentiation, Montgomery proposed to use an alternative representation of integers modulo n, called *Montgomery reduction* [Mon85]. It allows to carry out the modular multiplication without performing the classical modular reduction step. Instead, the more efficient Montgomery reduction is applied.

While the costs of solving the time-lock puzzle in an optimal way are well known, the release time will vary depending on the speed of the recipient's processor and is somewhat coarse-grained. However, Rivest argues that the speeds of hardware available to consumers differ only by a small constant factor and even the power of high-end hardware available to companies is usually within the same order of magnitude due to non-parallelizability of the problem. We agree on this rationale and further investigate it by comparing the puzzle solution times on different off-the-shelf machines. Our offline submission protocol tolerates authors with slower machines if they start to solve their puzzle at some time before the deadline.

6.1.2 More Timed-Release Cryptography

In [Mao01], Mao developed a zero-knowledge protocol which enables Alice to prove to Bob that a *timed encryption* or a *timed signature* based on time-lock puzzles can be actually unlocked by performing t modular squarings. Boneh and Naor [BN00] introduced a verifiable timed commitment scheme extending the standard notion of commitments. It adds a potential forced opening phase which permits the receiver to recover with some effort the committed value without the help of the committer. Like in time-lock puzzles, the recovery rests upon repeated squaring. Possible applications for timed commitments are contract signing, honesty-preserving auctions, and concurrent zero-knowledge. Building on the work of Boneh and Naor, Garay and Jakobsson proposed a timed release scheme for standard digital signatures—RSA, Schnorr, and DSA [GJ03].

A different approach to timed-release cryptography that does not require the receiver to solve a puzzle and provides fine-grained timing is presented by Blake and Chan [BC05]. They assume a trusted time server which periodically broadcasts signed time-bound key updates I_t to the users. The time server does not need to interact with either the

Chapter 6 Offline Submission with RSA Time-Lock Puzzles

sender or the receiver and is therefore passive. At release time t the receiver can decrypt his message by means of I_t. This scheme is based upon a bilinear pairing. Cathalo et al. [CLQ05] improved it by introducing a new stringent security model and strengthening the anonymity of receivers. Other contributions to timed-release cryptography using trusted time servers are, e. g., [COR99, DY05, CHVSn07]. In contrast, we pursue an offline approach and cannot rely on or even assume the presence of a trusted time server.

6.2 RSA Time-Lock Puzzle Scheme

6.2.1 Key Generation

We incorporate the time-lock puzzle mechanism into the default RSA public-key cryptosystem and make the puzzle non-interactive. The resulting scheme is called *RSA time-lock puzzle*. Everyone who knows Alice's public puzzle key can solve a puzzle by encrypting an arbitrarily chosen message m. The puzzle complexity is determined by the size of Alice's public key. Alice constructs her RSA puzzle key pair with the artificially enlarged public key by performing the following steps:

1. Generate at random two large primes p and q of equal bit-length (e. g., 1024 bits).

2. Compute the modulus $n = pq$ and Euler's totient function $\varphi(n) = (p-1)(q-1)$.

3. Randomly choose a private exponent d, $1 < d < \varphi(n)$, such that $gcd(d, \varphi(n)) = 1$ and determine its multiplicative inverse modulo $\varphi(n)$: $e = d^{-1}\ mod\ \varphi(n)$.

4. Choose the puzzle difficulty t which is the number of modular squarings Bob has to perform to solve the puzzle, i.e., to carry out the public-key operation. Suppose that a high-performance reference machine can do S squarings modulo n per second and a public-key operation shall take T seconds, then $t = T \cdot S$.

5. Compute the remainder
$$r = 2^t\ mod\ \varphi(n) \tag{6.3}$$
and the public exponent
$$\tilde{e} = 2^t + \varphi(n) - r + e. \tag{6.4}$$

$z = \varphi(n) - r + e$ denotes the lower bits of $\tilde{e}$ which are preceded by a long sequence of 0-bits and finally the leading 1-bit at position t.

6. $(n, \tilde{e})$ is the public and (n, d) the private key. Since $\tilde{e}$ is an extremely large number with lots of 0-bits after the leading 1-bit, the public key can be efficiently represented by storing the triple (n, t, z). In binary, z is at most twice as long as n.

The inflated public exponent $\tilde{e}$ is constructed by adding a large multiple of $\varphi(n)$ to the regular exponent e. It holds that $m^e \equiv m^{\tilde{e}} \pmod{n}$ for all $m \in \mathbb{Z}_n$, since $e \equiv \tilde{e} \pmod{\varphi(n)}$ and n is a product of distinct primes. $\tilde{e}$ has been chosen to be the smallest appropriate exponent which is larger than 2^t. The time to perform the modular reduction of 2^t in step 5 depends, of course, on the puzzle difficulty t. However, even when creating a puzzle with a solution time in the order of several days, step 5 will take only a few minutes.

6.2.2 Public and Private Key Operation

Solving a puzzle for a context m, $0 < m < n$, chosen by the solver Bob means to carry out the public-key operation by encrypting m with Alice's public key $(n, \tilde{e})$ in the usual manner, i.e., to compute the ciphertext

$$c = m^{\tilde{e}} \bmod n. \tag{6.5}$$

Due to the special structure of $\tilde{e}$, the fastest way to perform this giant modular exponentiation is to solve the actual puzzle

$$\alpha = m^{2^t} \bmod n \tag{6.6}$$

in T seconds by repeated squaring and to quickly do the regular-sized modular exponentiation

$$\beta = m^z \bmod n \tag{6.7}$$

which yields

$$c = \alpha \cdot \beta \bmod n. \tag{6.8}$$

Chapter 6 Offline Submission with RSA Time-Lock Puzzles

Bob submits the pair (m, c), i.e., the context and the corresponding puzzle solution, to Alice. She verifies the solution by applying her private key (n, d) in the usual manner to decrypt the ciphertext and to compare the result with m:

$$c^d \bmod n \stackrel{?}{=} m. \tag{6.9}$$

Since d is of regular size, this operation takes just a few milliseconds. If the verification succeeds, Alice is convinced that Bob has spent about T seconds to solve the puzzle (or even longer, if his computer ist not as fast as Alice's high-end reference machine).

6.2.3 Security Analysis

The security of our RSA puzzle scheme can be reduced to the security of Rivest's puzzle construction. It must be impossible for Bob to compute c without performing the t modular squarings in Equation 6.6. Determining $\varphi(n)$ in order to reduce $\tilde{e}$ to e is provably as hard as factoring n and therefore is not an option. Bob knows 2^t, $\tilde{e} = 2^t + z$ and $z = \varphi(n) - r + e$ respectively, but has no information about the individual summands $\varphi(n)$, $-r$, and e. With regard to $\varphi(n)$ and $r = 2^t \bmod \varphi(n)$, the case is the same as in Rivest's scheme. Being the modular inverse of the randomly generated number d, e is completely random as well and therefore is not correlated with either $\varphi(n)$ or r. Thus, we cannot identify $\varphi(n)$ or r from z. The only possibility remaining is to determine e from z if some information on the relationship between $\varphi(n)$ and r is known. Suppose Bob can easily find the difference $\varphi(n) - r$, then Rivest's scheme would be broken as well. In this case Bob would be able to compute

$$y = a^{\varphi(n)-r} \bmod n = a^{-r} \bmod n = (a^r)^{-1} \bmod n \tag{6.10}$$

and to determine the puzzle solution $a^{2^t} \bmod n$ by inverting y modulo n. For the very unlikely case that y is not invertible, i.e., $y \notin \mathbb{Z}_n^*$, $gcd(y, n) = p$ or $gcd(y, n) = q$ and we have factored n.

It is crucially important that after publishing $\tilde{e}$ Alice never reveals for the same key pair another exponent $\hat{e}$, e.g., a smaller one to make the puzzle easier. Otherwise the modulus n could be factored quite quickly. $\delta = \tilde{e} - \hat{e}$ is a multiple of $\varphi(n)$ and there exists an efficient randomized algorithm which allows to factor n if a multiple of $\varphi(n)$ is given [Kra86]. Though the algorithm requires to perform at least one modular exponentiation with an exponent in the order of δ, i.e., takes about as long as solving one instance of the puzzle, knowing the factorization of n enables to solve all future puzzles instantly.

6.2.4 Delayed Encryption and Signature Verification

Our RSA time-lock scheme can be used not only to solve puzzles, but also to delay the regular RSA encryption and signature verification process. Using the public exponent $\tilde{e}$ instead of e the public-key operation will take about T seconds where T can be chosen arbitrarily. What is this good for? We propose two possible applications.

The first one is a well-known certificate authority which decides to provide its services for advertising purposes free of charge or a for very low fee, if the certificate holders accept a restriction on the computational speed of their public key. Companies and large organizations usually do not bother about the certification fee and buy a full-fledged certificate. Thus, the primary target group would be individuals and small societies who often cannot afford to pay the regular fee. Instead of limiting the validity of a trial certificate to some days which makes it actually useless, the CA would accept only artificially enlarged public exponents for long-term certification within the promotion. It could prescribe to provide a public exponent of the form $2^t + z$ where t is chosen as large as to perform the public-key operation in not less than T seconds. Reasonable values for T may be, e.g., 60 seconds for a free and 10 seconds for a low-fee certificate. Such an overhead when encrypting a message for the certificate holder or verifying his signature would not constitute a serious limitation for parties with whom individuals or small societies usually communicate. The proposed marketing strategy would make the CA even more popular and leverage the deployment of public-key cryptography.

The second application focuses on delayed signature verification in the context of contract signing. In a company only very few persons should be authorized signatories, i.e., possess the company's private key enabling them to sign arbitrary contracts on behalf of the company. Besides the CEO, there may be only one deputy who has access to the private key and even he may not enjoy the CEO's full confidence. The CEO will

Chapter 6 Offline Submission with RSA Time-Lock Puzzles

be keen on to restrict the deputy's signing capability but must pay attention not to compromise the company's capacity to act in case of his sudden absence or illness. Our approach to this dilemma is for the CEO to generate two key pairs and to certify for his company two public keys. The first and regular public key is of normal size while the second one is an artificially enlarged puzzle key (n, t, z) and takes, e.g., $T = 48\ h$ per operation. The private key corresponding to the regular public key would be known solely to the CEO, while the second private key is disclosed to the deputy. Computing a signature is an easy task with both private keys. However, only a signature created with the CEO's private key can be efficiently verified. Under normal circumstances all current contracts are signed by the CEO and the other party can immediately check the signature. Concluding an agreement with the deputy is not attractive due to the extremely time-consuming signature verification. But in case that the CEO is temporarily not available, the only way to stay in business is for the deputy to sign the pending contract and for the other party to be patient while validating the signature. Except for this inconvenience, the other party receives a full-fledged signature which, if necessary, can be presented in court. It will take the court once again time T to check the signature, but this is not an issue. As soon as the CEO is available, he may resign the contract with his private key yielding a quickly verifiable signature. Holding a private key whose genuineness cannot be easily validated, the deputy is much less vulnerable to attempts to rapidly extort the key under threat of violence than the CEO. Under the condition that the deputy does not know $\varphi(n)$, which he does not need to know to generate signatures, the hijackers would have to wait for time T to test whether the revealed private key is actually genuine. Instead, in case of sharing the regular private key, both the CEO and his deputy would be worthwhile targets.

6.2.5 Other Applications for RSA Time-Lock Puzzles

Generally speaking, the solution of an RSA time-lock puzzle constitutes a non-interactive and non-parallelizable proof of work for an arbitrarily chosen context m that took (at least) time T. Beyond the offline submission that we present in the next section, one could make use of RSA puzzles to enable an ordinary citizen to get an appointment with a high-ranking politician, e.g., a mayor or a minister, and to discuss a crucial concern m. By solving a long-term puzzle for m the citizen demonstrates that he really has a strong intention and deserves to be listened to. This increases his chances for getting a time-slot for the concern m—and only for it.

6.2.6 Small Private Exponent

To speed up the private key operation, the private exponent d can be chosen considerably smaller than the modulus n. Boneh and Durfeecite [BD00] showed that as long as $d < n^{0.292}$, one can break RSA by recovering the private exponent from the public key. However, this attack on small private exponents is only feasible if the public exponent $e < n^{1.875}$. Hence, since our RSA puzzle scheme relies on an extremely large public exponent, Boneh's attack does not apply here. Of course, d must be chosen large enough that it cannot be guessed by brute force. A minimal size in the same order of magnitude as symmetric keys seems to be appropriate, e.g., 128–192 bits.

6.3 Offline Submission Protocol

Based on the RSA time-lock puzzle scheme, we propose now an offline submission protocol which enables an author currently being offline to commit to its ready-made document before the deadline and to submit it at some time past the deadline upon regaining connectivity. The goal is to convince the accepting institution of the timely completion of the document by means of a successfully solved RSA puzzle.

6.3.1 Basic Design

The institution generates an RSA puzzle key pair where the public-key operation takes time T on a reference machine being equipped with a state-of-the-art high-end processor. It can perform S modular squarings per second and should be one of the fastest systems available on the market to end users. Setting the bar high is important to ensure that nobody can gain a time advantage over other authors who submit in time. The institution publishes the public puzzle key (n, t, z) in the usual fashion, e.g., by requesting a certificate from a trusted CA and making it available on its website and in public-key directories. An author intending to submit a document obtains the puzzle

Chapter 6 Offline Submission with RSA Time-Lock Puzzles

certificate in advance—just in case he has no Internet connection to the submission server when the deadline approaches. Many different scenarios are conceivable, ranging from hardware or ISP failure, a cable break, a DoS attack on the submission server to a location-dependent unavailability of Internet access in a remote region.

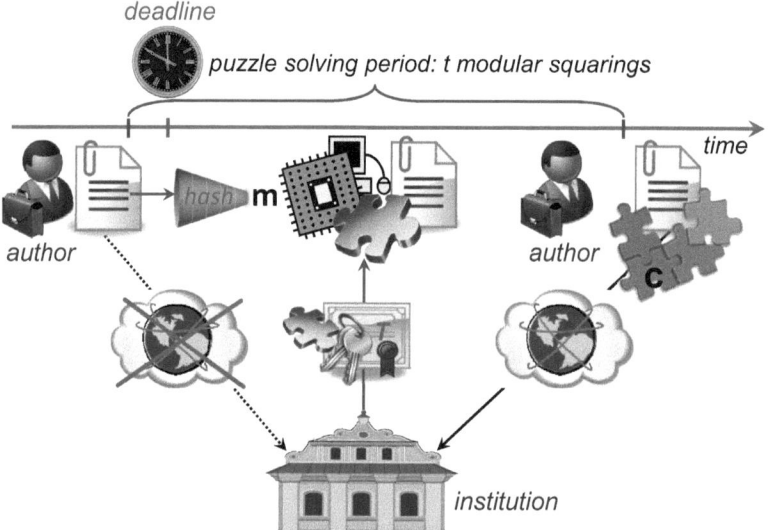

Figure 6.1: Illustration of the offline submission protocol.

Should this be the case, the author begins to solve an RSA puzzle for his document. Note that electricity to run the computer is usually available even in an adverse environment. He applies a cryptographic hash function (e.g., SHA-1 or RIPEMD-160) to his document producing a digest which serves as input m for the puzzle. Figure 6.1 illustrates the offline submission scenario. If his computer is as fast as the reference machine, he computes the solution $c = m^{\tilde{e}} \bmod n$ in time T. Assuming that at that time the Internet connection to the server is available again, the author finally submits its document along with the puzzle solution c. Now the institution verifies the solution by decrypting c with its private key and matching the result against the document's hash value: $c^d \bmod n \stackrel{?}{=} m$. If the validation succeeds, the institution is convinced that the author has finalized his document at least T seconds ago. Is this point in time before the deadline, the submission can be predated and accepted. It is up to the institution to specify a maximum submission delay beyond which no documents can be considered any more due to the closure of the review process.

In case that the author holds a slower processor than the reference machine, he can compensate for this handicap by beginning to solve the puzzle at some point before the deadline—ideally, just after the finalization of the document. Let S' denote the number of modular squarings that the author's machine can perform per second, then he must start solving a puzzle designed for T seconds at least $(\frac{S}{S'} - 1)T$ seconds before the deadline to succeed.

6.3.2 Building a Puzzle Chain

In practice, the author cannot predict exactly when he regains connectivity to the submission server. Solving a single but very complex puzzle which probably takes more time than the period without Internet access lasts would be suboptimal, especially for owners of older hardware. Therefore we propose for the institution to issue several public puzzle keys with different levels of difficulty, e.g., one for 12 hours, for 4 hours, for 1 hour, and one for 10 minutes. The author can estimate the anticipated offline time and begins to solve the most suitable puzzle. If he is still offline after having solved the first puzzle, he continues to solve puzzles by building up a *puzzle chain*: The solution c_1 of the first puzzle becomes the input m_2 of the second, usually shorter lasting puzzle. The author continues to chain up his puzzle solutions according to this scheme until he finally regains connectivity to the server after k puzzle steps. Then he can submit his document along with the k chain links $c_1, ..., c_k$. Each solution should bear a label stating the public key used. The institution now validates the chain by verifying each puzzle solution: $c_i^{d_i} \mod n_i \stackrel{?}{=} m_i$ for $1 \leq i \leq k$ where $m_1 = m$ and $m_i = c_{i-1}$ for $i > 1$. Note that this task can be performed in parallel. Summing up the times T_i assigned to the utilized public keys yields the total time by which the submission is predated.

6.3.3 Alternative Approach

Another approach for solving the puzzle only as long as necessary is for the author to choose the large exponent for the computation by himself. He could simply compute $c = m^{2^t} \mod n$ by repeated squaring for a t which is as large as he actually needs, i.e., the final t would be the number of modular squarings performed until the Internet connection becomes available again. This approach would ignore the RSA property of the original puzzle construction and require only the modulus n along with the speed indication S from the reference machine. The institution would need to compute $r = 2^t \mod \varphi(n)$ first prior to verifying $m^r \mod n \stackrel{?}{=} c$. A drawback of this scheme is the relatively expensive modular reduction of 2^t which must be rerun for each submitted puzzle instead of performing it only once during the key generation. Moreover, in the modular exponentiation $m^r \mod n$ the exponent r is roughly the same size as n, while in the RSA puzzle scheme a smaller private exponent d can be chosen, see Section 6.2.6. Verifying a short chain of RSA puzzles is therefore several orders of magnitudes faster.

6.4 Implementation and Evaluation

6.4.1 The OSRTLP Tool

We have implemented a platform-independent tool in C++, called $OSRTLP$[1], which performs all parts of our offline submission protocol. It is available for free download including the sources (with Visual C++ project, GNU Makefile, and precompiled binaries for Windows) [Jerb]. At the beginning, the institution can use OSRTLP for running a puzzle benchmark on a high-end reference machine to determine the number of modular squaring operations S executed per second. Next, it creates an RSA key pair with a public puzzle key taking T seconds per operation. Both the modulus size n and puzzle time T can be chosen arbitrarily. OSRTLP outputs the puzzle's private key and a puzzle certificate in X.509 v3 format containing, besides subject information and public puzzle key, the puzzle time T. It is signed by the institution's CA private key. If necessary, the institution may ask a well-known CA to cross-certify its CA public key. The author

---
[1]This is the acronym for *Offline Submission with RSA Time-Lock Puzzles*.

6.4 Implementation and Evaluation

utilizes OSRTLP to solve a puzzle for his document by supplying the institution's puzzle certificate. It can be verified by OSRTLP against a trusted CA certificate (or even a chain). At first, OSRTLP performs a short benchmark to inform the user about the time expected to finish the puzzle and indicates the current progress in percent. One can choose between the hash functions SHA-1, SHA-256 and RIPEMD-160. While solving the puzzle, OSRTLP periodically backups the intermediate result to a file and can simply resume the computation in case of a crash. Finally, the institution runs OSRTLP to quickly verify the solution for a submitted document by applying the puzzle's private key.

For the large-integer arithmetic we employ the open source library *MPIR* [MPI] which is a fork of the well-known *GMP* library from GNU [GMP]. GMP claims to be faster than any other bignum library by using fast algorithms with highly optimized assembly code. This serves our needs very well since we aim to provide a puzzle solver which cannot be easily outperformed. The institution must have confidence that the author is not able to solve the puzzle quicker than supposed, at least not at an acceptable price. MPIR / GMP implements several state-of-the-art multiplication algorithms, ranging from the base-case schoolbook method to the Karatsuba, Toom-Cook, and FFT algorithms. The choice depends on the bit length. For squaring integers which have the size of a typical RSA modulus, i.e., 1024–4096 bits, MPIR / GMP resorts to the schoolbook and Karatsuba method. The thresholds are platform-dependent. On current CPUs, for integers larger than 1536–1920 bits Karatsuba'a algorithm, running in $\mathcal{O}(N^{1.585})$, outperforms the basecase $\mathcal{O}(N^2)$ method. N denotes the number of machine words (in practice, 32 or 64 bits long) required to represent the integer. For repeated modular squaring we make use of Montgomery reduction instead of performing the classical reduction by dividing. This speeds-up the puzzle solution by a factor of 1.3–2.0, especially for small moduli in the order 1024–2048 bits. The private key operation for puzzle verification is also optimized by performing two exponentiations modulo p and q and afterwards applying the Chinese Remainder Theorem which yields the solution modulo n.

All MPIR / GMP functions operate on integers which are completely stored in memory. However, 2^t is far too large to be held in memory and consists almost only of zeros. To perform the modular reduction $r = 2^t \bmod \varphi(n)$ we have therefore modified the library's division routine to efficiently represent the dividend by occupying storage space only in

Chapter 6 Offline Submission with RSA Time-Lock Puzzles

the order of the modulus (i.e., the divisor). The same issue arises when storing the public exponent $\tilde{e} = 2^t + z$ in an X.509 certificate. We address it by encoding $\tilde{e}$ as the odd integer $E = z \cdot 2^{65} + t \cdot 2^1 + 1$ where t is represented as a 64-bit integer. Such a puzzle time-lock certificate can be distinguished from a regular one by a time-lock indication in the subject alternative name extension.

In Section 4.4.1, we have brought up the implementation of fast modular exponentiation on FPGAs and modern GPUs. They do not significantly surpass modern CPUs. While a GPU implementation of the puzzle solver may be a reasonable extension of our OSRTLP tool, we believe that the great majority of authors would not buy expensive special purpose hardware like FPGAs for offline submission.

6.4.2 Extensions: GUI and Online Submission System

In a bachelor thesis [Röm11], we have extended OSRTLP by a user-friendly GUI with wizard-style interface to support authors in solving puzzles. The GUI has been implemented using the open-source cross-platform *Qt framework* [Qt] for C++ and thus is available for all current platforms ranging from Windows to Linux and Mac OS. By resorting to a list of puzzle certificates with public keys having different levels of difficulty the new application automatically builds a puzzle chain to bridge an arbitrary long time gap. The author may specify a lower threshold for the anticipated offline period and update it at runtime to keep the length of the puzzle chain short. Figure 6.2 shows the new OSRTLP application running in GUI mode. It creates a puzzle chain and currently solves a puzzle with $T = 3\ min$. Moreover, the application can automatically check whether Internet connectivity has become available again and upload the document to the submission server through a HTTP (or HTTPS) POST request. To emphasize the practical feasibility of our scheme, we have also incorporated the offline submission protocol into a PHP-based Web submission system for homework assignments [Röm11]. It enables students to submit their homework even after the deadline if they attach a puzzle chain that proves the timely completion of their work. The submission server runs OSRTLP to verify the puzzles and calculate the time credit. If the validation succeeds, the submitted homework assignment gets accepted, is stored in the database and forwarded to a tutor.

6.4 Implementation and Evaluation

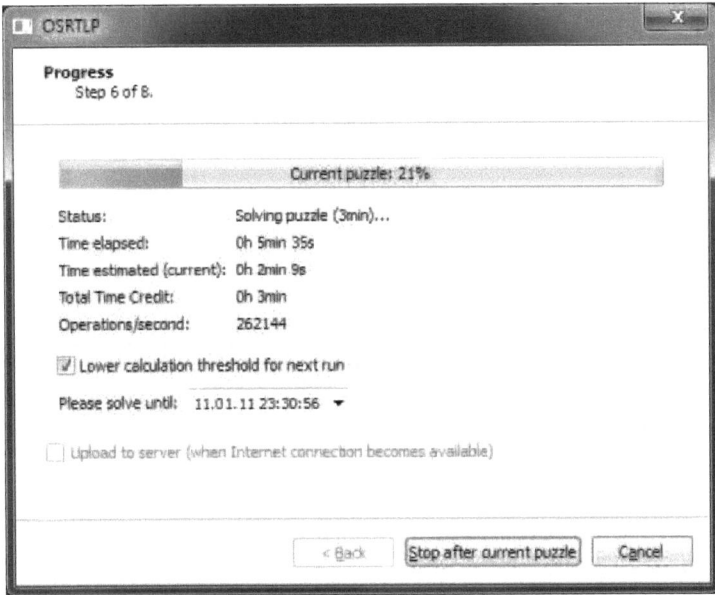

Figure 6.2: OSRTLP GUI with wizard-style interface: solving a puzzle chain [Röm11].

Chapter 6 Offline Submission with RSA Time-Lock Puzzles

6.4.3 Performance Evaluation

We run OSRTLP in benchmark mode on different platforms to measure the number of modular squaring operations S that each machine can perform per second. Our goal is to compare to what extent the puzzle solution time differs between an up-to-date high-end CPU being a candidate for the reference machine and a processor that was purchased some years ago. We also investigate the difference between 32-bit and 64-bit architectures and the impact of the operating system. We compiled OSRTLP and MPIR 1.3.1 with GCC 4.4.1 on Linux and Visual C++ 2008 SP-1 on Windows. The results for 1024, 2048, and 4096 bit moduli, all averaged over multiple runs, are shown in Table 6.1. To make it easier putting in relation the different CPUs, we state their release date as well as the manufacturer's release price (in 1000-unit quantities).

Evaluating the results, two main observations can be made: First, a 64-bit implementation of OSRTLP outperforms its 32-bit counterpart by a factor of 3.4–4.0. Consequently, in the face of the performance achievable on a 64-bit platform, running a 32-bit version of OSRTLP is not an option. Since all desktop CPUs manufactured during the last six years are 64-bit capable and 64-bit operating systems are widely available, this is in fact not an issue. Second, the difference in speed between 64-bit platforms, ranging from a 5.5 years old Core 2 Duo E6400 2.13 GHz, a 4 years old high-performance Xeon X3360 2.83 GHz to a 3 years old Core 2 Duo T9900 3.06 GHz costing 530 $ at release time, amounts to no more than factor 1.5. For the majority of users holding an up-to-date computer the gap between the reference CPU and their own CPU will be actually smaller. This result strongly supports our assumption that non-parallelizable puzzles constitute a feasible approach to measure how much time must have elapsed since the beginning of the computation. Another observation is that the choice of the operating system hardly influences the runtime of the puzzle.

The time required for the institution to perform the modular reduction $r = 2^t \bmod \varphi(n)$ when creating the public puzzle key is indicated in Table 6.2. It is proportional to the desired puzzle solution time T. For a long-term puzzle of several days' duration it takes only a few minutes. The larger the modulus n, the faster the computation of r takes since S decreases for increasing n more quickly than the division speed.

Table 6.1: Performance comparison of the modular squaring operation on different platforms.

platform	CPU release date & price		S: modular squarings/sec		
			1024 bits	2048 bits	4096 bits
Intel Core 2 Duo E6400 2.13 GHz Linux 2.6.31 64-bit	07/2006	183 $	941 320	261 750	71 340
Intel Core 2 Duo E6750 2.66 GHz Windows 7 32-bit			290 420	80 790	21 520
Windows 7 64-bit	07/2007	183 $	1 161 860	323 410	87 880
Linux 2.6.31 32-bit			328 670	94 340	26 360
Linux 2.6.31 64-bit			1 174 160	324 670	88 590
Intel Core 2 Quad Q9400 2.66 GHz Linux 2.6.31 64-bit	08/2008	183 $	1 180 970	326 250	88 810
Intel Core 2 Duo T9900 3.06 GHz Linux 2.6.31 64-bit	04/2009	530 $	1 396 290	386 330	104 780
Intel Xeon X3360 2.83 GHz Linux 2.6.31 64-bit	03/2008	266 $	1 237 160	346 730	93 940
AMD Athlon II X2 240e 2.80 GHz Linux 2.6.31 64-bit	10/2009	77 $	1 092 270	345 080	99 600

Table 6.2: Computation time of $r = 2^t \mod \varphi(n)$ on an Intel Core 2 Duo E6750 2.66 GHz for different puzzle difficulties $t = T \cdot S$ with an Intel Core 2 Duo T9900 3.06 GHz as reference machine for S.

puzzle time T	modulus size n		
	1024 bits	2048 bits	4096 bits
10 min	0.754 sec	0.292 sec	0.132 sec
1 h	4.512 sec	1.738 sec	0.791 sec
12 h	53, 98 sec	20, 91 sec	9.50 sec
24 h	108.0 sec	41, 84 sec	18.98 sec
72 h	324.2 sec	125.7 sec	56.93 sec

6.5 Chapter Summary

In this chapter, we have introduced a non-interactive and non-parallelizable RSA time-lock puzzle scheme. By artificially enlarging the public exponent the time required to encrypt a message can be arbitrarily tuned. Based on RSA time-lock puzzles, we have proposed an offline submission protocol. It enables an author currently being offline to commit to its document before the deadline and to submit it at some time past the deadline upon regaining connectivity. Presenting the correct solution of a puzzle with assigned solution time T proves to the institution that the submitted document has been finalized at least time T ago. In practice, several puzzles with different solution times are chained up to bridge an arbitrary long time gap while the author is offline. We have implemented a platform-independent tool performing all parts of our offline submission protocol and evaluated the variance of the solution time between different platforms. It turned out to be fairly low. Furthermore, we have set up a Web submission system for homework assignments which incorporates our offline submission protocol and thus demonstrates the practical feasibility of our approach.

Chapter 7

Conclusion

In this thesis, we have devised techniques and protocols to mitigate and ideally to prevent denial-of-service attacks in local area networks. The goal was to make communication in LANs secure and DoS-resistant. Our contribution began with a comprehensive link layer security protocol that employs public-key cryptography. However, public-key operations are relatively expensive compared to symmetric-key primitives and protocols relying on them may be vulnerable to DoS attacks. It is known that performance is the price to pay for security and usability. But we were convinced that it must be possible to provide DoS resistance and stability without compromising security or cutting back usability.

The *Cryptographic Link Layer (CLL)* introduced in Chapter 2 was the starting point on the way to safe communication in LANs. It provides authentication and confidentiality to neighboring hosts from layer 2 upwards. Each machine holds a certificate and is identified by its IP/MAC address pair. CLL safeguards all unicast IP traffic by means of a block cipher and a message authentication code. Furthermore, CLL extends ARP and DHCP handshakes with authentication and thus protects these protocols against various kinds of attacks. Beginning with an ARP handshake, two hosts exchange certificates and cryptographic parameters, authenticate each other using public-key cryptography, and negotiate symmetric keys to establish a security association. CLL is transparent to existing protocols and has been implemented for both Windows and Linux. It achieves wire-speed throughput in 100 Mbit Ethernet and provides a competitive throughput rate even in Gigabit Ethernet.

In Chapter 3, we have presented *counter-flooding*—a countermeasure against DoS flooding attacks to protect public-key handshakes in LANs and, in particular, CLL's ARP

Chapter 7 Conclusion

handshake. Exploiting the lack of initial address authenticity, the attacker tries to sabotage the public-key handshake between two hosts A and B by overwhelming B with fake signature packets. In the counter-flooding approach, the benign host A reacts to this aggression by flooding itself multiple copies of its signature packet for a short period while the victim host B first collects all incoming signature packets during a given time period. It then verifies only a fixed number of signatures per period without becoming overloaded and selects those packets for verification that have the largest number of duplicates. Under weak assumptions we have shown how host A can ensure that its signature packet will be among the packets selected for verification. The applicability of our defense scheme has been supported by flooding experiments where we studied the bandwidth division between concurrent flows under overload conditions. Thus, somewhat surprisingly, we can successfully combat the attacker using his own weapons.

A different DoS countermeasure that has been widely discussed in the literature are client puzzles. In Chapter 4, we have first highlighted the drawbacks of existing client puzzle schemes, especially if being applied in LANs. The main issue of interactive client puzzles is their vulnerability to DoS counterattacks on the clients, which results from missing authentication of the puzzle parameters. Then we have introduced a novel client puzzle scheme that is based on the computation of square roots modulo a prime and offers some advantages over existing approaches. *Modular square root puzzles* are non-parallelizable, provide polynomial granularity, have compact solution and verification functions, and can be employed both interactively and non-interactively. In LANs, we argued for constructing non-interactive client puzzles in order to render counterattacks impossible. Resorting to the counter-flooding idea, we have also incorporated a small bandwidth-based cost factor for the client into our scheme to raise its efficiency. Benchmark results demonstrated the feasibility of our approach to mitigate DoS attacks on hosts in 1 or even 10 Gbit networks.

In the *secure client puzzle architecture* in Chapter 5, we have provided a solid basis to safely employ non-interactive client puzzles. It overcomes the authentication issue of interactive puzzles without tolerating precomputation attacks. The key idea is to derive puzzles from a periodically changing, secure random beacon. The beacons are generated in advance for a longer time span and broadcasted in the LAN by a special beacon server. To authenticate the beacon packets, the hosts obtain a signed fingerprint package which contains the cryptographic digests of the beacons. Beacon verification is cheap and can be performed at line speed, since it requires only a single hash operation. A server suffering from DoS accepts requests only from those clients that have constructed and solved a fresh puzzle of sufficient difficulty from the current beacon. To provide a robust and secure beacon service, we have developed sophisticated techniques which address synchronization aspects and facilitate the deployment of beacon fingerprints. Even if hosts fail to obtain the signed fingerprint package using one of the regular distribution channels, they can acquire it on the fly from the beacon server and verify its signature despite of possible DoS flooding attacks.

Chapter 6, the final contribution of this thesis, pursued the idea of cryptographic puzzles beyond DoS protection and introduced a novel application in the area of timed-release cryptography. We have developed a non-interactive and non-parallelizable *RSA time-lock puzzle* scheme where the time required to encrypt a message can be arbitrarily tuned by artificially enlarging the public exponent. As with modular square root puzzles, this scheme also relies on the non-parallelizability of repeated squaring. The solution time cannot be shortened significantly by employing many machines and it varies only slightly across modern CPUs. Based on RSA time-lock puzzles, we have proposed a protocol for *offline submission*. It enables an author currently being offline to commit to its document before the deadline and to submit it past the deadline upon regaining connectivity. Having continuously solved an RSA puzzle (or a chain of puzzles) for his document during the offline period, the author finally presents the puzzle solution to the institution as a proof for the timely completion of his work. We have implemented a platform-independent tool that performs all parts of our offline submission protocol and set up a Web submission system for homework assignments which incorporates our protocol.

In summary, we have provided a comprehensive security protocol for LANs and developed multiple schemes to protect it as well as other protocols and services, especially those also relying on public-key cryptography, against DoS attacks. We have looked at the attacker's abilities and counteracted with the controlled emission of packets and the solution of puzzles. Secure and DoS-resistant LAN communication is possible. We are convinced that some of the techniques proposed in this thesis can be also applied in the Internet and future protocol designs will benefit from them.

Bibliography

Own Publications

[JLSM08] Yves Igor Jerschow, Christian Lochert, Björn Scheuermann, and Martin Mauve. CLL: A Cryptographic Link Layer for Local Area Networks. In *SCN 2008: Proceedings of the 6th Conference on Security and Cryptography for Networks*, pages 21–38, September 2008.

[JM10] Yves Igor Jerschow and Martin Mauve. Offline Submission with RSA Time-Lock Puzzles. In *CIT 2010: Proceedings of the 10th IEEE International Conference on Computer and Information Technology*, pages 1058–1064, June 2010.

[JM11] Yves Igor Jerschow and Martin Mauve. Non-Parallelizable and Non-Interactive Client Puzzles from Modular Square Roots. In *ARES 2011: Proceedings of the 6th International Conference on Availability, Reliability and Security*, pages 135–142, August 2011.

[JM12a] Yves Igor Jerschow and Martin Mauve. Modular Square Root Puzzles: Design of Non-Parallelizable and Non-Interactive Client Puzzles. *Elsevier Computers & Security*, 2012. Submitted for publication.

[JM12b] Yves Igor Jerschow and Martin Mauve. Secure Client Puzzles based on Random Beacons. In *IFIP Networking 2012: Proceedings of the 11th International Conference on Networking*, pages 184–197, May 2012.

[JSLM06a] Yves Igor Jerschow, Björn Scheuermann, Christian Lochert, and Martin Mauve. A Cross-Layer Protocol Evaluation Framework on ESB Nodes (Demo). In *REALMAN '06: Proceedings of the 2nd International Workshop on Multi-hop Ad Hoc Networks: from Theory to Reality*, pages 104–106, May 2006.

[JSLM06b] Yves Igor Jerschow, Björn Scheuermann, Christian Lochert, and Martin Mauve. A Real-World Framework to Evaluate Cross-Layer Protocols for Wireless Multihop Networks. In *REALMAN '06: Proceedings of the 2nd International Workshop on Multi-hop Ad Hoc Networks: from Theory to Reality*, pages 1–6, May 2006.

Bibliography

[JSM09]   Yves Igor Jerschow, Björn Scheuermann, and Martin Mauve. Counter-Flooding: DoS Protection for Public Key Handshakes in LANs. In *ICNS 2009: Proceedings of the 5th International Conference on Networking and Services*, pages 376–382, April 2009.

Other References

[ABMW05]   Martin Abadi, Mike Burrows, Mark Manasse, and Ted Wobber. Moderately Hard, Memory-bound Functions. *ACM Transactions on Internet Technology*, 5:299–327, May 2005.

[AK88]   Leonard Adleman and Kireeti Kompella. Using Smoothness to Achieve Parallelism. In *STOC '88: Proceedings of the 20th Annual ACM Symposium on Theory of Computing*, pages 528–538, 1988.

[AKO+04]   Hayriye Altunbasak, Sven Krasser, Henry Owen, Joachim Sokol, Jochen Grimminger, and Hans-Peter Huth. Addressing the Weak Link Between Layer 2 and Layer 3 in the Internet Architecture. In *LCN '04: Proceedings of the 29th Annual IEEE International Conference on Local Computer Networks*, pages 417–418, November 2004.

[AKZN05]   J. Arkko, J. Kempf, B. Zill, and P. Nikander. SEcure Neighbor Discovery (SEND). RFC 3971, March 2005.

[AMM77]   Leonard Adleman, Kenneth Manders, and Gary Miller. On taking roots in finite fields. In *SFCS '77: Proceedings of the 18th Annual Symposium on Foundations of Computer Science*, pages 175–178, September 1977.

[ANL01]   Tuomas Aura, Pekka Nikander, and Jussipekka Leiwo. DOS-Resistant Authentication with Client Puzzles. In *Revised Papers from the 8th International Workshop on Security Protocols*, pages 170–177, April 2001.

[Ant]   Antidote. http://antidote.sourceforge.net.

[Arp]   ArpWatch. http://ee.lbl.gov and http://freequaos.host.sk/arpwatch.

[Bac02]   Adam Back. Hashcash - A Denial of Service Counter-Measure, August 2002. http://www.hashcash.org/papers/hashcash.pdf.

[BC05]   Ian F. Blake and Aldar C-F. Chan. Scalable, Server-Passive, User-Anonymous Timed Release Public Key Encryption from Bilinear Pairing. In *ICDS 2005: Proceedings of the 25th International Conference on Distributed Computing Systems*, pages 504–513, June 2005.

Bibliography

[BCK96] Mihir Bellare, Ran Canetti, and Hugo Krawczyk. Message Authentication Using Hash Functions: the HMAC Construction. *RSA CryptoBytes*, 2(1), 1996.

[BD00] Dan Boneh and Glenn Durfee. Cryptanalysis of RSA with Private Key d Less than $N^{0.292}$. *IEEE Transactions on Information Theory*, 46(4):1339–1349, 2000.

[BN00] Dan Boneh and Moni Naor. Timed Commitments. In *CRYPTO '00: Proceedings of the 20th Annual International Cryptology Conference on Advances in Cryptology*, pages 236–254, August 2000.

[BOR03] D. Bruschi, A. Ornaghi, and E. Rosti. S-ARP: a Secure Address Resolution Protocol. In *ACSAC '03: Proceedings of the 19th Annual Computer Security Applications Conference*, pages 66–74, December 2003.

[BS96] Eric Bach and Jeffrey Shallit. *Algorithmic Number Theory, Volume I: Efficient Algorithms*. MIT Press, 1996.

[BT09] Kemal Bicakci and Bulent Tavli. Denial-of-Service attacks and countermeasures in IEEE 802.11 wireless networks. *Computer Standards & Interfaces*, 31(5):931–941, September 2009.

[BWK00] Brahim Bensaou, Yu Wang, and Chi Chung Ko. Fair medium access in 802.11 based wireless ad-hoc networks. In *MobiHoc '00: Proceedings of the 1st ACM Interational Symposium on Mobile Ad Hoc Networking and Computing*, pages 99–106, August 2000.

[CHVSn07] Konstantinos Chalkias, Dimitrios Hristu-Varsakelis, and George Stephanides. Improved Anonymous Timed-Release Encryption. In *ESORICS 2007: Proceedings of the 12th European Symposium On Research In Computer Security*, pages 311–326, September 2007.

[Cip03] M. Cipolla. Un metodo per la risolutione della congruenza di secondo grado. *Rendiconto dell'Accademia Scienze Fisiche e Matematiche*, 9(3):154–163, 1903.

[CLQ05] Julien Cathalo, Benoît Libert, and Jean-Jacques Quisquater. Efficient and Non-interactive Timed-Release Encryption. In *ICICS 2005: Proceedings of the 7th International Conference on Information and Communications Security*, pages 291–303, December 2005.

[CLSY93] Jin-Yi Cai, Richard J. Lipton, Robert Sedgewickand, and Andrew Chi-Chih Yao. Towards uncheatable benchmarks. In *Proceedings of the 8th Annual Structure in Complexity Theory Conference*, pages 2–11, May 1993.

Bibliography

[CMMDM03] Máire McLoone Ciaran McIvor, John McCanny, Alan Daly, and William Marnane. Fast Montgomery Modular Multiplication and RSA Cryptographic Processor Architectures. In *Proceedings of the 37th Asilomar Conference on Signals, Systems, and Computers*, pages 379–384, November 2003.

[CMSW09] Liqun Chen, Paul Morrissey, Nigel P. Smart, and Bogdan Warinschi. Security Notions and Generic Constructions for Client Puzzles. In *ASIACRYPT '09: Proceedings of the 15th International Conference on the Theory and Application of Cryptology and Information Security*, pages 505–523, December 2009.

[Coh96] Henri Cohen. *A Course in Computational Algebraic Number Theory*. Springer, 1996.

[COR99] Giovanni Di Crescenzo, Rafail Ostrovsky, and Sivaramakrishnan Rajagopalan. Conditional Oblivious Transfer and Timed-Release Encryption. In *EUROCRYPT '99: Proceedings of the International Conference on the Theory and Application of Cryptographic Techniques*, pages 74–89, May 1999.

[CW03] Scott A. Crosby and Dan S. Wallach. Denial of Service via Algorithmic Complexity Attacks. In *SSYM'03: Proceedings of the 12th Conference on USENIX Security Symposium*, August 2003.

[DA01] R. Droms and W. Arbaugh. Authentication for DHCP Messages. RFC 3118, June 2001.

[DGN03] Cynthia Dwork, Andrew Goldberg, and Moni Naor. On Memory-Bound Functions for Fighting Spam. In *CRYPTO '03: Proceedings of the 23th Annual International Cryptology Conference on Advances in Cryptology*, pages 426–444, August 2003.

[DH76] Whitfield Diffie and Martin E. Hellman. New Directions in Cryptography. *IEEE Transactions on Information Theory*, IT-22(6):644–654, November 1976.

[DM04] Christos Douligeris and Aikaterini Mitrokotsa. DDoS attacks and defense mechanisms: classification and state-of-the-art. *Computer Networks*, 44(5):643–666, 2004.

[DMR06] Sujata Doshi, Fabian Monrose, and Aviel D. Rubin. Efficient Memory Bound Puzzles Using Pattern Databases. In *ACNS 2006: Proceedings of the 4th International Conference on Applied Cryptography and Network Security*, pages 98–113, June 2006.

[DN92] Cynthia Dwork and Moni Naor. Pricing via Processing or Combatting Junk Mail. In *CRYPTO '92: Proceedings of the 12th Annual International Cryptology Conference on Advances in Cryptology*, pages 139–147, August 1992.

Bibliography

[DR06] T. Dierks and E. Rescorla. The Transport Layer Security (TLS) Protocol Version 1.1. RFC 4346, April 2006.

[Dro97] R. Droms. Dynamic Host Configuration Protocol. RFC 2131, March 1997.

[DS01] Drew Dean and Adam Stubblefield. Using Client Puzzles to Protect TLS. In *SSYM'01: Proceedings of the 10th Conference on USENIX Security Symposium*, August 2001.

[DY05] Yevgeniy Dodis and Dae Hyun Yum. Time Capsule Signature. In *FC '05: Proceedings of the 9th International Conference on Financial Cryptography and Data Security*, pages 57–71, March 2005.

[Ett] Ettercap. http://ettercap.sourceforge.net.

[FKFL05] Wu-chang Feng, Ed Kaiser, Wu-chi Feng, and Antoine Luu. The Design and Implementation of Network Puzzles. In *INFOCOM 2005: Proceedings of the 24th IEEE Conference on Computer Communications*, pages 2372–2382, March 2005.

[Fle07] Sebastian Fleissner. GPU-Accelerated Montgomery Exponentiation. In *ICCS '07: Proceedings of the 7th International Conference on Computational Science*, pages 213–220, May 2007.

[Ger12] Moritz Gericke. *Parallelisierungsmechanismen für eine kryptographische Sicherungsschicht*. Institute of Computer Science, Heinrich Heine University, Düsseldorf, January 2012. bachelor thesis. http://www.cn.uni-duesseldorf.de/publications/library/Gericke2012a.pdf.

[GH03] Mohamed G. Gouda and Chin-Tser Huang. A secure address resolution protocol. *Computer Networks*, 41(1):57–71, 2003.

[GJ03] Juan A. Garay and Markus Jakobsson. Timed Release of Standard Digital Signatures. In *FC 2002: Proceedings of the 6th International Conference on Financial Cryptography*, pages 168–182, March 2003.

[GKTV04] Carl A. Gunter, Sanjeev Khanna, Kaijun Tan, and Santosh S. Venkatesh. DoS Protection for Reliably Authenticated Broadcast. In *NDSS '04: Proceedings of the Network and Distributed System Security Symposium*, February 2004.

[GMP] GMP: GNU Multiple Precision Arithmetic Library. http://gmplib.org.

[GN12] Maria Garnaeva and Yury Namestnikov. DDoS attacks in H2 2011, February 2012. http://www.securelist.com/en/analysis/204792221/DDoS_attacks_in_H2_2011.

[Gor98] Daniel M. Gordon. A Survey of Fast Exponentiation Methods. *Journal of Algorithms*, 27(1):129–146, 1998.

Bibliography

[HGS+08]   Helmut Hlavacs, Wilfried N. Gansterer, Hannes Schabauer, Joachim Zottl, Martin Petraschek, Thomas Hoeher, and Oliver Jung. Enhancing ZRTP by using Computational Puzzles. *Journal of Universal Computer Science*, 14(5):693–716, 2008.

[HW09]   Owen Harrison and John Waldron. Efficient Acceleration of Asymmetric Cryptography on Graphics Hardware. In *AFRICACRYPT '09: Proceedings of the 2nd International Conference on Cryptology in Africa*, pages 350–367, June 2009.

[IEE]   IEEE 802.1AE. Media Access Control (MAC) Security. http://www.ieee802.org/1/pages/802.1ae.html.

[IEE04a]   IEEE 802.11i-2004. Amendment 6: Medium Access Control (MAC) Security Enhancements. IEEE Standard, July 2004.

[IEE04b]   IEEE 802.1X-2004. Port Based Network Access Control. IEEE Standard, December 2004.

[IEE05]   IEEE 802.3-2005. Part 3: Carrier Sense Multiple Access with Collision Detection (CSMA/CD) access method and physical layer specifications, Annex 31B. IEEE Standard, December 2005.

[JB99]   Ari Juels and John G. Brainard. Client Puzzles: A Cryptographic Countermeasure Against Connection Depletion Attacks. In *NDSS '99: Proceedings of the Network and Distributed System Security Symposium*, pages 151–165, February 1999.

[Jera]   Yves Igor Jerschow. The CLL service & toolkit for Windows and Linux. http://www.cn.uni-duesseldorf.de/projects/CLL.

[Jerb]   Yves Igor Jerschow. The OSRTLP Tool: Offline Submission with RSA Time-Lock Puzzles. http://www.cn.uni-duesseldorf.de/projects/OSRTLP.

[KO62]   A. Karatsuba and Y. Ofman. Multiplication of Many-Digital Numbers by Automatic Computers. *Doklady Akademii Nauk SSSR*, 145:293–294, 1962. (Translation in *Physics-Doklady*, 7:595-596, 1963).

[Kra86]   Evangelos Kranakis. *Primality and Cryptography*. John Wiley & Sons, Inc., 1986.

[Kra01]   Hugo Krawczyk. The Order of Encryption and Authentication for Protecting Communications (or: How Secure Is SSL?). In *CRYPTO 2001: Proceedings of the 21st Annual International Cryptology Conference*, pages 310–331, August 2001.

[KS05]   S. Kent and K. Seo. Security Architecture for the Internet Protocol. RFC 4301, December 2005.

Bibliography

[Kv10] Ghassan O. Karame and Srdjan Čapkun. Low-Cost Client Puzzles based on Modular Exponentiation. In *ESORICS 2010: Proceedings of the 15th European Symposium on Research in Computer Security*, pages 679–697, September 2010.

[Leh69] D. H. Lehmer. Computer technology applied to the theory of numbers. *Studies in Number Theory, Prentice Hall, Englewood Cliffs, NJ*, pages 117–151, 1969.

[LEM07] Wesam Lootah, William Enck, and Patrick McDaniel. TARP: Ticket-based Address Resolution Protocol. *Computer Networks*, 51(15):4322–4337, 2007.

[Llo] Jack Lloyd. Botan Cryptographic Library. http://botan.randombit.net.

[Mao01] Wenbo Mao. Timed-Release Cryptography. In *SAC 2001: Proceedings of the 8th Annual International Workshop on Selected Areas in Cryptography*, pages 342–357, August 2001.

[Mil76] Gary L. Miller. Riemann's hypothesis and tests for primality. *Journal of Computer and System Sciences*, 13(3):300–317, 1976.

[Mil92] David L. Mills. Network Time Protocol (Version 3) Specification, Implementation and Analysis. RFC 1305, March 1992.

[Mon] Massimiliano Montoro. Cain & Abel. http://www.oxid.it/cain.html.

[Mon85] Peter L. Montgomery. Modular Multiplication without Trial Division. *Mathematics of Computation*, 44:519–521, 1985.

[MPI] MPIR: Multiple Precision Integers and Rationals. http://www.mpir.org.

[MR04] Jelena Mirkovic and Peter Reiher. A Taxonomy of DDoS Attack and DDoS Defense Mechanisms. *ACM SIGCOMM Computer Communication Review*, 34(2):39–53, 2004.

[MvOV96] Alfred J. Menezes, Paul C. van Oorschot, and Scott A. Vanstone. *Handbook of Applied Cryptography*. CRC Press, 1996.

[MZS06] Ivan Martinovic, Frank A. Zdarsky, and Jens B. Schmitt. On the Way to IEEE 802.11 DoS Resilience. In *Proceedings of IFIP NETWORKING 2006, Workshop on Security and Privacy in Mobile and Wireless Networking*, May 2006.

[MZW+08] Ivan Martinovic, Frank A. Zdarsky, Matthias Wilhelm, Christian Wegmann, and Jens B. Schmitt. Wireless Client Puzzles in IEEE 802.11 Networks: Security by Wireless. In *WiSec '08: Proceedings of the ACM Conference on Wireless Network Security*, pages 36–45, March 2008.

Bibliography

[NBF96] Bradford Nichols, Dick Buttlar, and Jacqueline Farrell. *PThreads Programming: A POSIX Standard for Better Multiprocessing*. O'Reilly Media, 1996.

[NHSK09] Nozomu Nishihara, Ryuichi Harasawa, Yutaka Sueyoshi, and Aichi Kudo. A remark on the computation of cube roots in finite fields. Cryptology ePrint Archive, Report 2009/457, 2009. http://eprint.iacr.org/2009/457.

[Ope] OpenSSL: The Open Source toolkit for SSL/TLS. http://www.openssl.org.

[pca] pcap (packet capture): libpcap / WinPcap. http://www.tcpdump.org and http://www.winpcap.org.

[PCTS02] Adrian Perrig, Ran Canetti, J.D. Tygar, and Dawn Song. The TESLA Broadcast Authentication Protocol. *RSA CryptoBytes*, 5(2):2–13, 2002.

[PLR07] Tao Peng, Christopher Leckie, and Kotagiri Ramamohanarao. Survey of network-based defense mechanisms countering the DoS and DDoS problems. *ACM Computing Surveys*, 39(1):3, 2007.

[Plu82] David C. Plummer. Ethernet Address Resolution Protocol: Or converting network protocol addresses to 48.bit Ethernet address for transmission on Ethernet hardware. RFC 826, November 1982.

[Qt] Qt: cross-platform application and UI framework. http://qt-project.org.

[Rab80] Michael O. Rabin. Probabilistic algorithm for testing primality. *Journal of Number Theory*, 12(1):128–138, 1980.

[Res] NT Kernel Resources. WinpkFilter. http://www.ntkernel.com.

[Röm11] Julius Römmler. *Offline-Einreichung von Übungsaufgaben mittels RSA Time-Lock Puzzles*. Institute of Computer Science, Heinrich Heine University, Düsseldorf, January 2011. bachelor thesis. http://www.cn.uni-duesseldorf.de/publications/library/Roemmler2011a.pdf.

[RSA78] R. L. Rivest, A. Shamir, and L. Adleman. A Method for Obtaining Digital Signatures and Public-Key Cryptosystems. *Communications of the ACM*, 21(2):120–126, 1978.

[RSW96] Ronald L. Rivest, Adi Shamir, and David A. Wagner. Time-lock puzzles and timed-release Crypto. Technical report, Massachusetts Institute of Technology, Cambridge, MA, USA, 1996.

[Sei00] Rich Seifert. *The Switch book*. Wiley, 2000.

Bibliography

[SG08] Robert Szerwinski and Tim Güneysu. Exploiting the Power of GPUs for Asymmetric Cryptography. In *CHES '08: Proceedings of the 10th International Workshop on Cryptographic Hardware and Embedded Systems*, pages 79–99, August 2008.

[Sha72] D. Shanks. Five number-theoretic algorithms. In *Proceedings of the 2nd Manitoba Conference on Numerical Mathematics*, pages 51–70, 1972.

[Sor99] Jonathan P. Sorenson. A Sublinear-Time Parallel Algorithm for Integer Modular Exponentiation. In *Proceedings of the Conference on the Mathematics of Public-Key Cryptography*, pages 528–538, June 1999.

[Suz07] Daisuke Suzuki. How to Maximize the Potential of FPGA Resources for Modular Exponentiation. In *CHES '07: Proceedings of the 9th International Workshop on Cryptographic Hardware and Embedded Systems*, pages 272–288, September 2007.

[SvB07] Patrick Schaller, Srdjan Čapkun, and David Basin. BAP: Broadcast Authentication Using Cryptographic Puzzles. In *ACNS '07: Proceedings of the 5th International Conference on Applied Cryptography and Network Security*, pages 401–419, June 2007.

[TBFN07] Suratose Tritilanunt, Colin Boyd, Ernest Foo, and Juan Manuel González Nieto. Toward Non-parallelizable Client Puzzles. In *CANS 2007: Proceedings of the 6th International Conference on Cryptology & Network Security*, pages 247–264, December 2007.

[TJ10] Qiang Tang and Arjan Jeckmans. On Non-Parallelizable Deterministic Client Puzzle Scheme with Batch Verification Modes. Centre for Telematics and Information Technology, University of Twente, January 2010. http://doc.utwente.nl/69557/.

[Ton91] A. Tonelli. Bemerkung über die Auflösung quadratischer Congruenzen. *Göttinger Nachrichten*, pages 344–346, 1891.

[TTC] Test TCP (TTCP) - Benchmarking Tool for Measuring TCP and UDP Performance. http://www.pcausa.com/Utilities/pcattcp.htm.

[vABHL03] Luis von Ahn, Manuel Blum, Nicholas J. Hopper, and John Langford. CAPTCHA: Using Hard AI Problems For Security. In *EUROCRYPT '03: Proceedings of the 22nd International Conference on Theory and Applications of Cryptographic Techniques*, pages 294–311, May 2003.

[VP07] Eric Vyncke and Christopher Paggen. *LAN Switch Security*. Cisco Press, 2007.

[WJHF04] Brent Waters, Ari Juels, J. Alex Halderman, and Edward W. Felten. New Client Puzzle Outsourcing Techniques for DoS Resistance. In *CCS '04: Proceedings of the 11th ACM Conference on Computer and Communications Security*, pages 246–256, October 2004.

Bibliography

[WR03] XiaoFeng Wang and Michael K. Reiter. Defending Against Denial-of-Service Attacks with Puzzle Auctions. In *SP '03: Proceedings of the 2003 IEEE Symposium on Security and Privacy*, pages 78–92, May 2003.

[WR04] XiaoFeng Wang and Michael K. Reiter. Mitigating Bandwidth-Exhaustion Attacks using Congestion Puzzles. In *CCS '04: Proceedings of the 11th ACM Conference on Computer and Communications Security*, pages 257–267, October 2004.

[WR08] XiaoFeng Wang and Michael K. Reiter. A multi-layer framework for puzzle-based denial-of-service defense. *International Journal of Information Security*, 7:243–263, July 2008.

[WVB+06] Michael Walfish, Mythili Vutukuru, Hari Balakrishnan, David Karger, and Scott Shenker. DDoS defense by offense. In *SIGCOMM '06: Proceedings of the 2006 conference on Applications, technologies, architectures, and protocols for computer communications*, pages 303–314, September 2006.

[YL06] T. Ylonen and C. Lonvick. The Secure Shell (SSH) Protocol Architecture. RFC 4251, January 2006.

Index

Symbols

NC 59, 92
P 59, 92
P-complete 59, 92

A

address authenticity ... 1, 33, 35, 52, 73
ARP .... 3, 7, 9, 13, 15 f, 19, 27
ARP spoofing 7, 9, 13
attack model 2, 74
authentication 2 f, 7 – 12, 14, 16, 20, 22, 24, 35, 37, 52, 63, 72 f

B

bastion 53
beacon .... 4, 72, 75, 77 – 83
binary exponentiation .... 58 f, 92
block cipher 14, 18, 20, 30, 33, 37
boss / worker model 30
broadcast .. 12 f, 15, 17, 22, 34, 37 f, 44, 46, 49, 72, 77, 79, 82 f, 85

C

CAPTCHA 55
CBC 14
CEO 97
Cipolla-Lehmer 56, 58, 61
client puzzles .. 4, 35, 51 – 55, 60 – 64, 72, 74 ff
CLL 3, 7, 50, 86
confidentiality .... 2, 8 f, 14
contract signing 93, 97
counter-flooding 3, 33, 69
cube root modulo a prime 64
currency .... 2, 35 f, 39, 67

D

DDoS attack 1, 35
DHCP .... 3, 7, 10, 13, 23 ff
DHCP starvation attack 7, 13, 25
Diffie-Hellman . 14, 16, 21, 28, 35, 53, 63
DNS 7, 83, 89
DoS attack . 1, 7, 13, 33, 35 f, 49, 51, 60, 63, 74, 81 ff, 86, 89
DSA 37, 71

E

Ethernet .. 7, 11, 13, 15, 26 f, 30, 38, 40, 45 f, 49, 60, 67, 77
extended Riemann hypothesis 56

F

fairness .... 40, 42, 46 f, 89
flow control .... 34, 45 ff, 49
FPGA 67, 104

G

GPU 67, 104

H

handshake 13 – 16, 18 – 21, 27 f, 33, 35, 37, 51, 60
hash function 14, 18, 20, 33, 35, 43, 51, 60, 67, 72, 76, 78, 80, 83, 91, 100, 102
hash-reversal puzzles . 51, 53, 76, 85, 91
HMAC .... 14 f, 18, 20, 24, 30, 37

I

ICMP 27, 74

123

Index

IEEE 802.11 35
IEEE 802.11i 11, 33, 35
IEEE 802.1AE 11
IEEE 802.1X 33, 35
IEEE 802.3x 34, 45
intrusion detection system 9
IP 7, 60, 74, 77
IP address 7, 12, 74
IPsec 9, 14, 51, 83
IV 14

K

Karatsuba's algorithm 58, 103

L

Las Vegas algorithm 56
Legendre symbol 55
link layer 1, 9, 11
Linux .... 8, 10, 26 f, 80, 104, 106

M

MAC address ...7, 11 f, 17, 19, 23 f, 27, 35, 38, 46, 74
MACsec .... see IEEE 802.1AE
master key 14, 18, 24, 28
Miller-Rabin test 58
MiM attack 7, 14
Montgomery reduction 65, 92, 103
MTU .... 26, 40, 43, 46, 67, 71, 82 f
multicast 81

N

network layer 1, 9, 11
non-parallelizable .... 4 f, 52, 54, 59, 90 f
nonce 18, 20

O

offline submission 2, 5, 89
OSRTLP 102, 104, 106

P

parallelization 30, 53, 59

precomputation .... 4, 62 f, 72, 76, 81
public-key cryptography ...2, 8, 13, 33, 37, 51, 71, 83, 97

Q

quadratic non-residue .... 55 f, 60
quadratic residue .... 55 f, 60

R

renegotiation 21
repeated squaring 52, 54, 58 f, 91 ff, 95, 102
replay attack .. 10, 18, 20, 22, 25, 79, 84
router 1, 11, 20, 73
RSA time-lock puzzles 5, 90, 94
RSA 15 f, 22, 27, 37, 40, 54, 71, 84, 91, 94
RTT .... 28 ff

S

S-ARP 10
SA .... 13, 16, 18 f, 21
security association .... see SA
SEND 33
signature .... 13, 15 f, 22, 27, 33, 37 f, 40, 42, 55, 71, 78, 83 f, 86, 90, 93, 97
smurf attack 13
spam 55
speak-up 36
square root modulo a prime. 4, 52, 54 ff, 58, 61, 66, 77
square-and-multiply .... see binary exponentiation
SSH 9
SSL / TLS 9, 35, 51, 83
subset sum problem 54
switch .... 11, 34, 40, 42, 45 f

T

TARP 10
TCP .... 28, 33, 46 f, 49, 60, 83
time synchronization 18, 41, 79

124

time-lock puzzles .... 54, 90 ff
timed-release cryptography .. 5, 54, 91 ff
Tonelli-Shanks 56, 58

U

UDP 12, 60, 77, 82
unicast ... 12 – 15, 17, 20, 28, 46, 49, 82

W

Wi-Fi 1, 8, 11, 27
Windows .... 8, 26 f, 102, 104, 106
WPA 11
WPA2 .... *see* IEEE 802.11i

i want morebooks!

Buy your books fast and straightforward online - at one of world's fastest growing online book stores! Environmentally sound due to Print-on-Demand technologies.

Buy your books online at
www.get-morebooks.com

Kaufen Sie Ihre Bücher schnell und unkompliziert online – auf einer der am schnellsten wachsenden Buchhandelsplattformen weltweit! Dank Print-On-Demand umwelt- und ressourcenschonend produziert.

Bücher schneller online kaufen
www.morebooks.de

VDM Verlagsservicegesellschaft mbH
Heinrich-Böcking-Str. 6-8   Telefon: +49 681 3720 174   info@vdm-vsg.de
D - 66121 Saarbrücken   Telefax: +49 681 3720 1749   www.vdm-vsg.de

Printed by Books on Demand GmbH, Norderstedt / Germany